Exploring the
White House

Inside America's Most Famous Home

Exploring the White House

Inside America's Most Famous Home

KATE ANDERSEN BROWER

Quill Tree Books
An Imprint of HarperCollinsPublishers

Quill Tree Books is an imprint of HarperCollins Publishers.

Exploring the White House: Inside America's Most Famous Home
Text copyright © 2020 by Kate Andersen Brower
Interior illustrations © 2020 by Jennifer Hom
Residence map illustration by Molly Fehr
www.harpercollinschildrens.com
Library of Congress Control Number: 2020938936
ISBN 978-0-06-290642-7
Typography by Molly Fehr
22 23 24 25 26   PC/BRR   10 9 8 7 6 5 4 3 2 1

❖

First paperback edition, 2022

To my parents,
Christopher and Valerie Andersen,
who showed me the world

★ ★ ★
Contents

Living in the White House is like being on the stage, where tragedies and comedies play alternately. And we, the servants of the White House, are the supporting cast.

—LILLIAN ROGERS PARKS, *White House maid and seamstress from 1929 to 1961*

Introduction

Can you imagine what it would be like to live in the White House? The fifty-five-thousand-square-foot building located at 1600 Pennsylvania Avenue in the heart of Washington, D.C., is the country's most famous house. It has been home to forty-three presidents. Only George Washington missed out on living there, because it hadn't been built yet, and Grover Cleveland was the only president to leave and return for a second term four years later. So he was lucky that he got to live in the White House twice!

In 1800, President John Adams and First Lady Abigail Adams moved in. Since then, dozens of children have lived in the White House, and one baby was born there. (Esther Cleveland was born to President Cleveland and his wife, Frances, in 1893.)

It may seem glamorous, but it's not always easy to live in the public eye. Luci Baines Johnson, a daughter of Lyndon B. Johnson, who was president in the 1960s, called the White House "a public fishbowl" because she had almost no privacy and she felt like people could look in at her every move.

BEHIND THE SCENES

The White House is home to just one famous family at a time. The building is the country's most powerful and longest-lasting symbol of the presidency. The nation knows the residents of the White House—the first family—but few know about the dozens of people who work behind the scenes to keep the president's house running. The Residence staff rarely get any attention—in fact, most people have no idea they exist—and that's exactly how they like it.

The members of the building's supporting cast are its permanent employees: the approximately one hundred Residence workers who stay on from one administration to the next, regardless of political party. These are chefs, florists, ushers, housekeepers, butlers, engineers, painters, and more who work to make the White House comfortable for the first family.

They work long hours. They often sacrifice their personal lives to serve the first family with quiet, awe-inspiring dignity. They do not care if they are working for a Republican president or a Democrat; they treat every first family the same. It's not just a job—it's a calling, and many consider it an honor to serve.

MEET THE STAFF

I have been interested in the White House and the people who work and live there since I became a reporter for Bloomberg News during President Barack Obama's first four years in office. In my job as a reporter—which was very exciting!—I went on trips with the president and the first lady and traveled on the president's plane, which is called Air Force One (technically any plane the president is on should be called Air Force One, but really there are only two planes high-tech enough for the job. There are two planes so that one is always ready whenever the president needs it—even at the last minute.). When reporters travel with the president, they often become so distracted with the stories they are working on that they forget how historic it is to be sitting on that famous plane.

I can remember first hearing the giggles in the press cabin onboard the blue-and-white Boeing 747-200B as about twenty of my fellow reporters and I caught a glimpse of the Obamas' fluffy and playful Portuguese water dog running down the aisle from the front of the plane. The dog's name is Bo, and at the time he was just three years old and having fun on the country's most historic airplane. We all looked up from our laptops and our phones for a few wonderful minutes and took in the scene as a White House Residence staffer desperately tried to summon the rascally Bo—his white paws bounding up and down the aisle and his tongue and tail wagging happily—back to the front of the plane where his family was waiting for him. The Obamas were traveling to Martha's Vineyard for summer vacation and they brought their dog along for the ride. It was one of the rare moments when I caught a glimpse of the people who serve the first family but are rarely ever seen. It also reminded me that the president and his family are just like the rest of us—they like having their dog around to play with too, and sometimes their pets don't follow the rules either!

No matter what job you have someday, always be sure to take the time to look around you and soak in the special parts of it. In 2011, I was invited to a luncheon with First Lady Michelle Obama, along with about a dozen other reporters who covered the first lady. I was nervous, and excited! Lunch was served in the small and cozy Old Family Dining Room (it would be a huge room in any normal-size house, but everything in the White House is built on a grand scale, and this is one of the smaller rooms). It is also a private room tucked away from public view. I had never seen this private side of the White House. I didn't even know the room existed!

An elegantly dressed gentleman offered us champagne

on a gleaming silver tray and Michelle Obama called him by his first name. The menu included salad with vegetables from the White House garden—which the first lady had created—and fresh pan-roasted fish elegantly presented on the Truman china. (It's called the Truman china because the pattern for the dinnerware was picked out by President Harry Truman and his wife, Bess. In modern times most administrations choose their own china.) Each course was served by the butler, who clearly had a wonderful relationship with the first lady.

This is all very elegant, like being an English princess, I thought.

This experience, coupled with watching the aide try to convince Bo to head back to his seat on Air Force One, left me wondering—who were these people, so close to the world's most powerful family? So I made it a mission to find out who they were. Many people told me it would be impossible to get them to talk about their experiences, but they were wrong. Never let someone tell you that something can't be done! In my research, I interviewed dozens of current and former Residence staff who have devoted themselves to caring for the first families. They are the housekeepers and butlers, the chefs, florists, plumbers, and painters who are all incredibly proud of their work and who stay in their jobs for decades, serving the institution of the American presidency and not one particular president. They are not Democrats or

Republicans, they told me—they are Americans. This is an important and often ignored part of our incredible democracy and I'm excited for you to meet these loyal and hardworking people. Each staffer who has served at the White House has seen history, and each has incredible stories to tell. This book shares what they have taught me about the traditions and rituals of the White House, as well as some of what they have witnessed behind the scenes.

CHAPTER 1

1600 Pennsylvania Avenue:
The Most Famous House in the Country

Standing in front of 1600 Pennsylvania Avenue, the White House looks like a grand, three-story mansion. But it's really much more than meets the eye. The White House actually has eight floors—six full levels and two mezzanines, or partial floors. It boasts 132 rooms, 147 windows, 35 bathrooms, 28 fireplaces, 8 staircases, and 3 elevators!

And on these eight floors are some pretty unusual rooms, not normally found in a regular house. For example, while the main kitchen is located on the Ground Floor, there is also a Flower Shop and a Carpenter's Shop! The first floor—also called the State Floor—is the main level, where visitors can explore during guided tours. The Chief Usher's Office and the Pastry Kitchen are tucked in between the State Floor and the second and third floors, which are the first family's private quarters. There are also several levels of basements and underground spaces.

Each floor has a room shaped like an oval: the Diplomatic Reception Room on the Ground Floor (where President Franklin Delano Roosevelt delivered his fireside chats and where the first family usually enters the Residence); the Blue Room on the State Floor (which overlooks the South Lawn

History in Every Room

Special events have happened in almost every room of the White House. Consider the Lincoln Bedroom on the second floor. When Abraham Lincoln was president, it was actually his office and not his bedroom! In that room, Lincoln signed the Emancipation Proclamation, which freed slaves in the South in 1863. He said he had never "felt more certain that I was doing right, than I do in signing this paper." (It was a long process though, and slavery did not officially end until December 1865, when the Thirteenth Amendment to the Constitution ended slavery everywhere in the United States.) Lincoln's dedication to holding the country together and defeating slavery has made him one of the most important presidents in United States history. A copy of the legendary document can be found in the Lincoln Bedroom.

and features a beautiful glass French chandelier and vivid blue satin draperies); and the Yellow Oval Room on the second floor (which leads to the Truman Balcony).

There are four staircases in the Residence itself: the Grand Staircase, which goes from the State Floor to the private second floor; a staircase by the president's elevator, which goes from the basement to the third floor; a spiral staircase by the staff elevator, which goes from the first-floor mezzanine

Citizens would gather in the nearby Treaty Room and wait for a chance to meet with the president in his office. But Lincoln built a private passage so he could cut through the Treaty Room to go to his library in the Yellow Oval Room without dealing with the crowds waiting to see him. He walked right by his visitors, but because of a partition erected in the Treaty Room, they could not see him as he shuttled between his office (now the Lincoln Bedroom) and the Yellow Oval Room. He would see them when he was ready.

Citizens can no longer walk into the White House and visit with the president. Instead of serving as a public waiting room, the Treaty Room is now a private room and a presidential study. It got its name because a famous peace treaty with Spain was signed there in 1898. It is also where President John F. Kennedy signed the Limited Nuclear Test Ban Treaty in 1963.

Map of the Residence

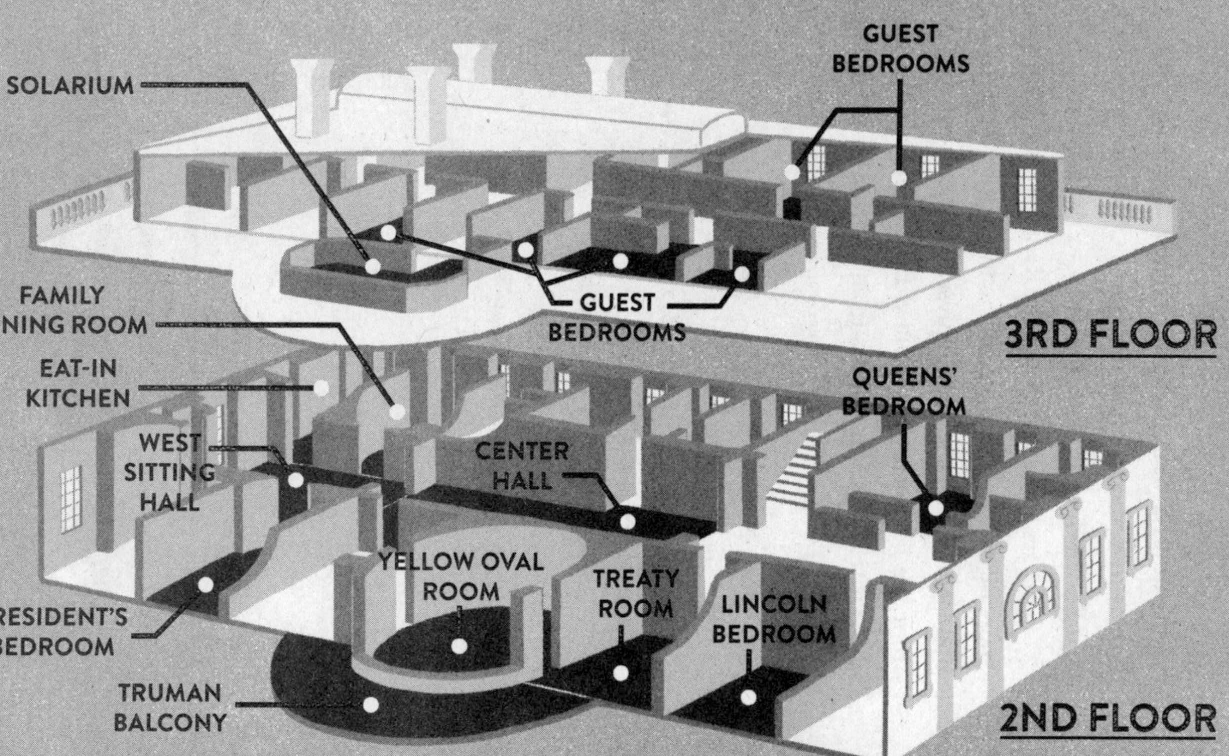

3RD FLOOR

GUEST BEDROOMS

GUEST BEDROOMS

SOLARIUM

FAMILY DINING ROOM

EAT-IN KITCHEN

WEST SITTING HALL

CENTER HALL

2ND FLOOR

QUEENS' BEDROOM

LINCOLN BEDROOM

TREATY ROOM

YELLOW OVAL ROOM

PRESIDENT'S BEDROOM

TRUMAN BALCONY

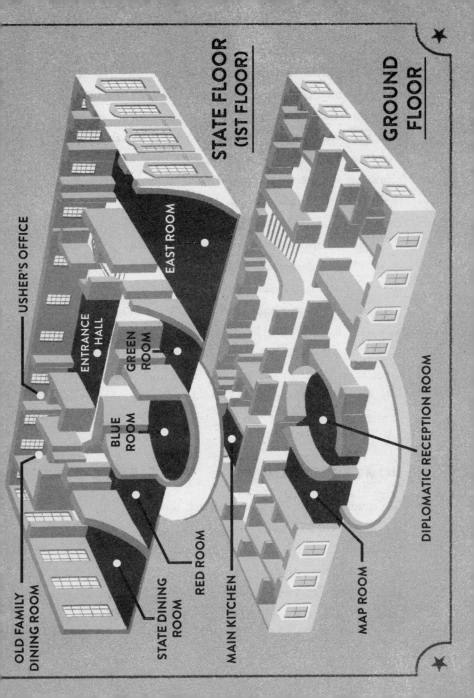

STATE FLOOR (1ST FLOOR)

GROUND FLOOR

USHER'S OFFICE

EAST ROOM

ENTRANCE HALL

GREEN ROOM

BLUE ROOM

OLD FAMILY DINING ROOM

STATE DINING ROOM

RED ROOM

MAIN KITCHEN

DIPLOMATIC RECEPTION ROOM

MAP ROOM

to the basement; and a fourth staircase—the true "back stairs"—which runs from the second floor by the Queens' Bedroom (an elegant rose-colored room named for royalty who have stayed there) to the east end of the third floor. Maids sometimes use this staircase if they need to clean rooms on the second floor and want to avoid interrupting the first family. It allows them to walk all the way up to the third floor and circle back down.

There are also secret rooms that most people don't talk about. The underground locker rooms where butlers keep their tuxedos and maids house their uniforms are just a short distance from a bomb shelter under the East Wing that was built for President Franklin Delano Roosevelt during World War II. This room is now the President's Emergency Operations Center, built to withstand a nuclear blast. It is a tube-shaped bunker where the president may be taken in case of an attack.

HOME SWEET HOME

But despite all these different official rooms, ultimately the White House is a home to the first family. "The White House is built on a human scale," said Tricia Nixon Cox, the eldest daughter of President Richard Nixon and First Lady Pat Nixon. One day, after a welcoming ceremony on the South Lawn, a visiting European prince turned to Tricia and said, "It really *is* a house." He had been astonished by the scale of the executive mansion compared with the palaces he knew. "To him, it looked small!"

The White House may be less imposing than some royal palaces, but it is far from modest. The large Entrance Hall on the north side opens to the eighty-foot-long East Room at one end and the State Dining Room, often used for state dinners in honor of foreign heads of state, at the other.

In fact, early presidents and first ladies complained that the house was too big. It was considered the largest house in the United States until after the Civil War. Around Inauguration Day, almost every guest room is crammed with friends and family.

Taxpayers spent about $230,000—roughly $4,380,000 in today's dollars—to build the White House. It is estimated to be worth about $300 million, although many would claim it is priceless.

In addition to its extraordinary and historic architecture, the White House is home to about thirty thousand historic objects, including paintings, furniture, and documents. It's both the president's house and a presidential museum!

THE PRIVATE SIDE

The family's private rooms on the second and third floors are linked by one main corridor on each floor. There are sixteen rooms and six bathrooms on the second floor and another twenty rooms and nine bathrooms on the third. Maids and valets have sometimes stayed on these floors, as well as presidential children.

The guest rooms do not have numbers on their doors, but they are known among the Residence staff by their room numbers, just like at a hotel. Every week, each of the White House maids is assigned a roster of rooms to clean.

BUILDING—AND REBUILDING—THE WHITE HOUSE

The White House was designed by the Irish-born architect James Hoban, after he won a competition held by the first president, George Washington, and his secretary of state, Thomas Jefferson. Washington chose the winning design from among six entries. (It is thought that Jefferson anonymously submitted a plan using the initials A. Z.) Hoban's design was inspired by Leinster House, an eighteenth-century

Georgian mansion in Dublin, Ireland, which is home to Ireland's parliament. Construction on the White House began in 1792.

In choosing Washington, D.C., as the site for the capital, George Washington had predicted that the city would someday rival the beauty of Paris and London, but at first Washington, D.C., lagged far behind such magnificent European capitals. It took time to envision and build a city!

During the initial construction of the White House, a stone yard was erected on the northeast side of the mansion with dozens of large sheds housing worktables used for cutting stone. Close to the new walls of the house were two tall tripod rigs for hoisting the stone blocks into place. The rigs supported huge pulleys—some as high as fifty feet—which loomed over the massive construction site. The stones were painted with a lime-based whitewash so that the porous material would not absorb water that could freeze and crack the stone. The White House wasn't painted bright white until 1818, though it had been known as the White House for

Fun Fact

Even though George Washington selected the site of the capital city and the site of the future White House, he is the only president to never have lived there because the White House was not yet finished when he died. The first president served his two terms in New York and Philadelphia.

years. President Theodore Roosevelt made the name official in 1901.

Despite the grandeur of its architecture, the White House would remain a very unglamorous place to live for decades after its first stone was laid. In 1800, when John Adams, the nation's second president, and his wife, Abigail, became the first residents of the White House, there were only six rooms suitable to live in. Their new home was far from complete, and Washington was such a swampy, isolated city that the first family had trouble even finding the house. They wandered for hours looking for it!

When they finally did find their way home, they had to walk on wooden planks to get through the front door, since the front steps had not yet been installed. They were basically living in a construction site. A laundry and horse stables were

Abigail Adams used the East Room to dry the laundry.

located in the area now occupied by the West Wing. The first lady hung wet laundry in the giant, empty East Room. The ceilings were more than twenty feet high, so she had plenty of room to spread out!

"We have not the least fence, yard, or other convenience," Abigail Adams wrote to her daughter. "The principal stairs are not up, and will not be this winter."

When the Adamses moved into the White House, Abigail estimated that she would need at least thirty servants to run the estate properly. The Adamses brought just four servants with them. In early administrations, it was up to the first families to bring their own maids, cooks, and valets, and they had to pay the personal staff themselves.

In recent decades, while some first families have brought a loyal employee or two from their prepresidential lives, they mostly rely on the expertise of the nearly one hundred Residence staff who work at the White House from one administration to the next.

BURNING DOWN THE HOUSE

On August 24, 1814, toward the end of the War of 1812, the British looted and burned the White House to the ground. First Lady Dolley Madison famously saved a portrait of George Washington by cutting it out of the frame, with the help of Paul Jennings, an enslaved African American man who worked in the White House at the time. They did this in a frenzy before fleeing the burning house. The fire was said to have been so fierce that it could be seen from fifty miles away! (Scorch marks from the fire can still be spotted on the stones under the north entrance.)

When peace was finally established again, President Madison asked architect Hoban to help rebuild the mansion, which had already become a national symbol.

Since then, each president has sought to leave his mark on the building. The White House was subjected to various changes during the Victorian era in the nineteenth century, when people liked lots of detailed and dark woodwork.

The first major change occurred in 1902, when President Theodore Roosevelt hired the then-famous New York architectural firm McKim, Mead & White to renovate the house, with the understanding that they were to maintain its original neoclassical style. This is around the time when President Roosevelt officially named the building the White House. Before then, it was sometimes called the executive mansion.

As part of the project, Roosevelt had the third story outfitted with guest rooms and tore down a series of giant glass conservatories—rooms used to grow fruits and flowers for the first family—to clear a path for the expansion known as the West Wing. Later that year, Roosevelt moved his office from the second floor of the Residence into the West Wing.

A few years later, President William Howard Taft added the Oval Office, which was completed in 1909. Today, the president and his advisers work in the West Wing. The president spends most of his day in the Oval Office.

REPAIRS NEEDED

As time passed, the White House needed more maintenance to keep it up and running. Significant repairs and renovations were done during the Truman administration in the late 1940s and early 1950s. At that time, the roof was caving in and the house was in danger of collapsing! Once, the first lady was hosting a tea for a group of women in the Blue Room and the chandelier—which was as big as a refrigerator—swayed wildly above them. In another incident, the leg of daughter Margaret Truman's piano actually plunged through the rotted flooring of her sitting room during a particularly spirited practice session!

As part of the repairs, President Truman replaced the mansion's original wood framing with a steel infrastructure. He also added a second-floor outdoor space overlooking the South Lawn, which became known as the Truman Balcony. Presidents and their families have since enjoyed this space, sometimes having lunch or dinner outside or stepping out onto the balcony to relax and breathe in some fresh air. The Truman family lived at the presidential guesthouse across the street known as Blair House during the construction.

The East Wing was also added during this period. But it wasn't until decades later that Rosalynn Carter, first lady and wife of President Jimmy Carter, established the Office of the First Lady in the East Wing in 1977. Today, the White House complex includes the Residence (where the first family lives), the West Wing (where the president's political advisers sit), the East Wing (where the first lady's offices are located), the Eisenhower Executive Office Building (where the vice president's offices are located and where other presidential aides work), the Treasury Building (where finance and tax departments are located), and Blair House.

The Residence feels "like a very, very fancy New York apartment," President Obama's personal secretary Katie Johnson said. "There's all this stuff going on outside and around but once you're inside, it's your home."

KEEPING UP WITH THE TIMES

Many rooms in the White House have changed their purpose over time. For example, long after Abigail Adams used

White House Area Map

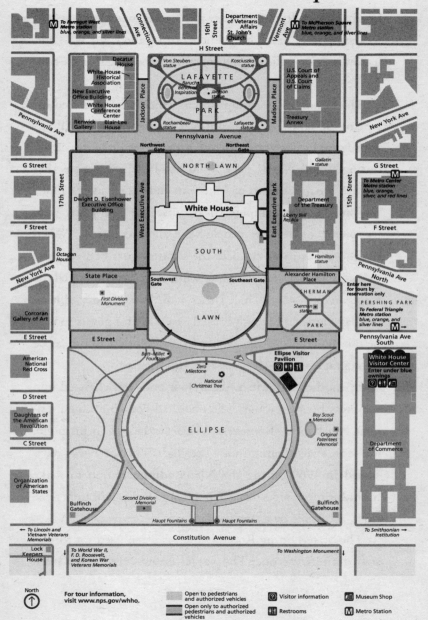

To Farragut West Metro station blue, orange, and silver lines

To McPherson Square Metro station blue, orange, and silver lines

Connecticut Ave

16th Street

Vermont Ave

Department of Veterans Affairs
St. John's Church

H Street

Decatur House

White House Historical Association

New Executive Office Building

White House Conference Center

Renwick Gallery

Blair-Lee House

Von Steuben statue

Kosciuszko statue

LAFAYETTE PARK

Baruch Bench of Inspiration

Jackson statue

Rochambeau statue

Lafayette statue

Jackson Place

Madison Place

U.S. Court of Appeals and U.S. Court of Claims

Treasury Annex

Pennsylvania Avenue

Pennsylvania Ave

New York Ave

G Street

G Street

17th Street

15th Street

Northwest Gate

Northeast Gate

NORTH LAWN

White House

West Executive Ave

East Executive Park

Dwight D. Eisenhower Executive Office Building

Gallatin statue

Department of the Treasury

Liberty Bell Replica

F Street

F Street

To Octagon House

SOUTH

Hamilton statue

New York Ave

Corcoran Gallery of Art

State Place

Southwest Gate

Southeast Gate

Alexander Hamilton Place

Pennsylvania Ave North

Enter here for tours by reservation only

SHERMAN

First Division Monument

LAWN

Sherman statue

PERSHING PARK

To Federal Triangle Metro station blue, orange, and silver lines

E Street

E Street

E Street

PARK

Pennsylvania Ave South

American National Red Cross

Butt-Millet Fountain

Zero Milestone

National Christmas Tree

Ellipse Visitor Pavilion

White House Visitor Center

Enter under blue awnings

D Street

Daughters of the American Revolution

Boy Scout Memorial

Original Patentees Memorial

C Street

ELLIPSE

Department of Commerce

Organization of American States

Second Division Memorial

Bulfinch Gatehouse

Bulfinch Gatehouse

To Lincoln and Vietnam Veterans Memorials

Haupt Fountains

Haupt Fountains

To Smithsonian Institution

Lock Keepers House

Constitution Avenue

To World War II, F. D. Roosevelt, and Korean War Veterans Memorials

To Washington Monument

North

For tour information, visit www.nps.gov/whho.

Open to pedestrians and authorized vehicles

Open only to authorized pedestrians and authorized vehicles

Security zone and gate

Visitor information

Restrooms

Refreshments

Museum Shop

Metro Station

it to hang and dry wet laundry, the East Room was converted to a temporary home for soldiers during the Civil War, and it now serves as the setting for most presidential press conferences.

The Ground Floor Map Room, which was once used for playing billiards, was transformed in the 1940s into President Franklin Delano Roosevelt's top secret planning center during World War II. The room was filled with maps that tracked the movements of American and enemy forces. (This was long before computers!) Because the war plans were top secret, only a few people were allowed inside. "When the room was to be cleaned, the security guard covered the maps with cloth, standing duty while the cleaner mopped the floor," remembered Chief Usher J. B. West. Today, during holiday parties, the room is used as a place for guests to wait before moving into the Diplomatic Reception Room to be photographed with the president and first lady.

In another big switch, the indoor pool was changed into the press briefing room. The pool had been built for President Franklin D. Roosevelt in 1933 to help with his polio, a disease that left him in a wheelchair. The space was redesigned in 1969 during the Nixon administration to make room for more reporters. (The empty pool is still under the floor, accessible by a trapdoor!)

The State Dining Room, which is often used for formal state dinners, was once Thomas Jefferson's office. The Green

Room, now a formal sitting room on the State Floor, began as Jefferson's bedroom and breakfast room, and James Monroe used it as a card parlor. The small Victorian-style Lincoln Sitting Room on the second floor was used as a telegraph room in the late nineteenth century. One president who particularly liked the Lincoln Sitting Room was Richard Nixon, who used it as a place to try to relax. Nixon liked the room's heavy drapes and dark furnishings, and he spent hours there with music blasting.

ON TOUR

The White House belongs to the nation, and the public can visit on tours. The White House is one of a few private residences of heads of state where the public can visit free of charge.

Every morning members of the staff roll out the carpets and hang ropes in the tour areas on the Ground Floor and State Floor so that as many as six thousand visitors can walk through. Every afternoon, after thousands of people have visited, the staff has to clean up so that if the first family wants to spend time on the State Floor, it won't look so much like a tourist destination. The house is back to being a private home again!

HOLIDAYS AT THE WHITE HOUSE

In addition to regular tours, the White House holds a number of special events around the holidays. During the holiday season, about seventy thousand people tour the White House to admire the festive decorations.

Another tradition is the White House Easter Egg Roll, held the Monday after Easter. It is the largest annual event at the White House. The first lady typically acts as hostess, often customizing the event to meet her vision. Some have added music or dancing.

The Easter celebrations began in the mid-1800s, when families picnicked and held egg hunts on the Capitol lawn. After a number of years,

A Calvin Coolidge Christmas

Congress banned the event because the festivities destroyed the grass. In response, President Rutherford B. Hayes invited the public to the White House lawn for a celebration, starting in 1878.

The egg hunt was canceled during World Wars I and II and during periods of construction, but the tradition was restarted in 1953. First Lady Pat Nixon introduced the White House Easter bunny for the first time in 1969. The tradition of receiving a wooden egg as a souvenir was started in 1981, during the administration of Ronald Reagan.

LIVING IN A NATIONAL PARK

Although state business and family living all happen in the White House, it is actually considered a national park, and many of the people who work there are National Park Service employees. The White House and grounds are part of President's Park, which includes eighty-two acres of parkland and gardens, as well as the White House itself.

The President's Park complex is home to Lafayette Square—a seven-acre public park north of the White House—as well as the Ellipse—a fifty-two-acre public park on the south side of the White House. These grounds have a long and storied history. Over the years, Lafayette Square has been used for many purposes, including a graveyard, a slave market, an encampment for soldiers during the War of 1812, and the site of many protests and celebrations.

The White House Rose Garden borders the Oval Office and has been the backdrop for many presidential announcements and meetings. It was established by Ellen Wilson, the first wife of Woodrow Wilson, in 1913. It replaced another garden created by Theodore Roosevelt's wife Edith in 1902.

Aerial view of the White House and the city of Washington, D.C.

WHERE DOES THE VICE PRESIDENT LIVE?

You may be asking yourself: Where does the vice president live in the White House? Well, actually, the vice president and the second family live at Number One Observatory Circle, a three-story, nine-thousand-square-foot house on the grounds of the U.S. Naval Observatory in Washington, D.C. It's not as fancy as the White House, but the 1893 house is not too shabby either.

It has been the official house of the vice president since 1974, but no one lived there at first. Gerald Ford was the first vice president eligible to live at the Observatory, but he assumed the presidency before renovations were completed.

The vice president's house is known to the White House staff as the VPR (vice presidential residence), or NAVOBS, short for its more formal name, the Naval Observatory.

Ford's vice president, Nelson Rockefeller, an heir to the Rockefeller fortune, used the house mainly to entertain. He had another, much fancier home nearby that he lived in! The first full-time vice presidential occupants of the Observatory were Walter Mondale, Jimmy Carter's vice president, and his wife, Joan, who took up residence there in 1977. Every vice president since has lived there. There are no public tours of the house, so fewer people know about it. In addition to having the vice president's residence on the grounds, the seventy-two-acre navy compound also provides astronomical and timing information used by the navy. And it has a world-class science library, including rare books by Galileo, Copernicus, Newton, and Einstein!

The vice president has an office in the West Wing, as well as offices in the Eisenhower Executive Office Building on the White House grounds.

CHAPTER 2
★ ★ ★

On the Job:
Working in the White House

There is a lot of work to be done to keep the White House running smoothly. Most of the job falls to the nearly one hundred permanent staff who work in the Residence. These employees are devoted to serving the president and first family. They are nonpartisan—they do not openly support any political party—and they act like professionals. They have a reputation for being discreet and proud of their work. Presidents come and go, but the Residence staff are the permanent fixtures of the White House.

GETTING ORGANIZED

Running the White House is like running a five-star hotel for the president of the United States and first lady. The fifty-five-thousand-square-foot, eight-floor house is kept in shape by a permanent team of people, including butlers, maids, chefs, and florists.

The chief usher is like the general manager of the hotel. This person oversees the entire operation, answering any concerns the president and the first lady might have about their home,

hiring staff, and managing the budget of about $13 million a year. Those funds go to the staff salaries and supplies, as well as the cost of heating, air-conditioning, and lighting the building. (Another $750,000 is set aside to repair and restore the White House every year.) When First Lady Jacqueline Kennedy lived in the White House in the 1960s, she called Chief Usher J. B. West "the most powerful man in Washington, next to the president."

It's not surprising that of the last three chief ushers, two managed hotels and one was in the military. U.S. Coast Guard Rear Admiral Stephen Rochon was appointed chief usher by President George W. Bush in 2007, becoming the first African American to serve in the role. President Barack Obama and First Lady Michelle Obama named Angella Reid to the position in 2011, making her the first woman and the second African American to hold the job. She had been the former general manager of the Ritz-Carlton in Arlington, Virginia, a suburb of Washington, D.C. President Donald

Trump and First Lady Melania Trump named Timothy Harleth as chief usher in 2017; he was the director of rooms at the Trump International Hotel in Washington, D.C.

Every person on the staff plays an important role in making things run smoothly. Here is a rundown of some of the key staff positions.

Ushers: In addition to the chief usher, who basically runs the show—and is the CEO of the Residence—assistant ushers and their aides oversee each department. They report to the chief usher and work out of a small office on the State Floor. Approximately four duty ushers run the desk in the Usher's Office and handle day-to-day activities.

Executive housekeeper: Oversees about twenty maids, including several "housemen," who move heavy furniture so the maids can clean the Residence.

Executive chef: Oversees several cooks in the White House main kitchen.

Executive pastry chef: Responsible for baking and desserts. The Pastry Kitchen is separate from the main kitchen and is located on one of the mezzanines.

Maître d', or head butler: Oversees about six full-time butlers who work in the second- and third-floor private quarters of the White House. Dozens of part-time butlers are also hired for state dinners and other large events.

Chief florist: Oversees a team of florists in the Flower Shop.

Valets: There are usually three valets who are military personnel who take care of the president's clothes, run errands, shine shoes, press shirts, and work with the housekeepers.

Head plumber: Oversees plumbers and works in the Plumbing Shop in the basement.

Chief engineer: Oversees engineers who work out of an office in the bottom basement. Engineers are in charge of all the mechanical work in the White House.

Chief electrician: Oversees electricians who do everything from rehanging priceless chandeliers to changing light bulbs.

Head painter: Painting the White House requires many gallons of paint, giant cranes, and a large staff. Being a painter at the White House means learning how to operate these big cranes to paint its seventy-foot exterior.

Head of the storeroom: Keeps the first family's fridge stocked. Takes an unmarked Secret Service van to a local grocery store to buy food for the president and first family. This top secret operation is done so that no one will try to tamper with the first family's food supply.

Chief curator: Oversees several curators who treat the White House like a museum. Curators are in charge of cataloging and protecting every piece of furniture and artwork in the White House's private collection, ranging from masterpieces by the famous portrait artist John Singer Sargent to porcelain dating back to George Washington.

Groundskeepers: The White House sits on eighteen acres in the middle of Washington, D.C. The groundskeepers maintain it very carefully, including its tennis court and swimming pool on the South Lawn. Mowing the enormous North and South Lawns takes eight hours—that's a full workday! Dale Haney has been the head groundskeeper for decades, and because he is a dog lover, he is also in charge of White House pups. He started taking care of Richard Nixon's Irish setter, King Timahoe, in the 1970s. He loved walking the Bushes' and the Obamas' dogs too.

Who's Who at the White House?

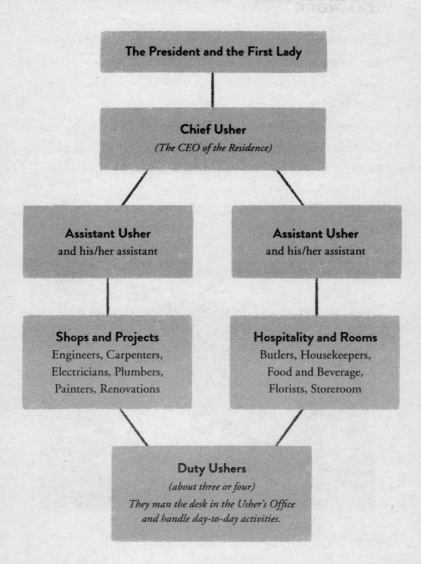

The President and the First Lady

Chief Usher
(The CEO of the Residence)

Assistant Usher
and his/her assistant

Assistant Usher
and his/her assistant

Shops and Projects
Engineers, Carpenters,
Electricians, Plumbers,
Painters, Renovations

Hospitality and Rooms
Butlers, Housekeepers,
Food and Beverage,
Florists, Storeroom

Duty Ushers
(about three or four)
*They man the desk in the Usher's Office
and handle day-to-day activities.*

This is approximate and can change from administration to administration.

TEAMWORK

"The White House staff works together to keep the operation going smoothly and the Residence looking as perfect as possible," said Bob Scanlan, who worked in the Flower Shop from 1998 to 2010.

"If a flower was down in an arrangement, it wasn't unusual for the housekeeper to come in and say, 'You guys might want to take a look at the Red Room, there are petals on the table. I picked them up but it looks like they're dropping still,'" Scanlan said. "We kept an eye out for each other because everything reflects on everybody."

Florist Bob Scanlan at work in the Flower Shop

Scanlan, who retired in 2010, said he misses the White House every day. "It's almost like an addiction," he said. "When you leave you have to wean yourself off of it. It's not only about the place, it's about the people too."

The White House employs a team of florists, led by a chief florist, who prepare arrangements daily in the Flower Shop, located in a small space on the Ground Floor, nestled under the driveway of the White House's North Portico.

In the early days of the White House, fresh flowers were on display only when they were in season during the summer months. Sometimes wax fruit or silk flowers were used for decoration. In the 1830s, greenhouses were installed and more fresh flowers were used. At the turn of the century, fresh flowers were brought in from other greenhouses in the area, and when air transportation became common, flowers were flown in on a more regular basis. The position of chief floral designer was created during the Kennedy administration.

Did You Know?

Harriet Lane, the niece of President James Buchanan, was the first person to bring fresh flowers into the White House. President Buchanan then ordered a conservatory be built on the west side of the White House so Harriet could choose what flowers she wanted. Lane was also the first person to be referred to as the "first lady." She accompanied Buchanan—the only lifelong bachelor to be president—to events and helped run the Residence. In 1858, *Harper's Weekly* referred to Lane as "Our Lady of the White House," and two years later, in *Frank Leslie's Illustrated Newspaper*, her picture was printed with this caption: "The subject of our illustration . . . . may be justly termed the first lady in the land."

Today, approximately five White House florists are responsible for coming up with unique arrangements that suit the first family's taste. During the holidays and in preparation for state dinners, the florists call in volunteers to help. The chief florist focuses on the public spaces and helps oversee all the arrangements.

Members of the Flower Shop share responsibility for decorating the entire complex, from the private quarters on the second and third floors to the West Wing, the East Wing, and the public rooms. No corner of the White House is overlooked.

"When you become part of that house and you are a florist, there's a certain element and a certain look that belongs strictly for that house," Scanlan said. "It's not just the first family's, it's the public's too. We're doing flowers for the country."

Reid Cherlin, who was a spokesman for President Obama, remembered being impressed by their work. "What always struck me was the flowers," Cherlin said. "Coming in in the morning in the West Wing, if you came in at the right time, the florists would be putting new bowls of peonies out," he said. "There's something about putting fresh flowers in a place where no one is necessarily going to be. It's one thing for them to be on the coffee table in the Oval Office, it's another thing to be sprucing things up in areas where people aren't even going to congregate."

HELP WANTED

From the highest staff position to the most entry-level post, getting hired to work at the White House is not as simple as answering an ad or applying online. "The jobs in the White House are not advertised," said Tony Savoy, head of the Operations Department from 1984 until 2013. His biggest responsibility was moving the first family into and out of the White House. "Nearly everyone I interviewed had a family member or a friend who recommended them for the job." The person making the referral was vouching for the integrity—and the ability to protect the first family's privacy—of the person they were suggesting be hired. Getting a job in the White House really is all about who you know!

Sometimes more than one member of a family worked at 1600 Pennsylvania Avenue. One family—the Ficklins—had *nine* family members work in the White House!

Often those hired stay on for decades, some even for generations. Part of that longevity on the job is because the staff becomes like a family, looking out for each other and caring for each other. They also have lots of fun together.

CHAPTER 3
★ ★ ★

True Professionals:
Loyalty to the First Family

The White House staff works around the president and first family every day, and over time many become friends and trusted allies. They learn to anticipate what the family wants even before they know it themselves.

They see what goes on behind the scenes and get to know the family's personal preferences and personalities, but—most important—they respect the family's privacy.

Staff members mind their own business: they do their jobs and understand that they are not to discuss what they see or hear that is intended to be

> **FUN FACT**
>
> John and Abigail Adams employed John Briesler as their steward for almost twenty years. Briesler and his wife, Esther, were the core staff at the White House. In total, there were only four servants!

private. Their goal is to help the first family live as normally as possible in the White House, and that includes the right to be themselves in their own home. The first family lives in a museum—one that offers daily tours—and yet they need some private space. Just imagine if you had someone listening in on every conversation in your house!

It takes a special kind of person to work at the White House. They must possess qualities of loyalty, devotion, and discretion. The Residence staffers do not work for the president but for the *institution* of the presidency. "Somehow you learn to separate the politics from the house," a current staffer said.

Did You Know?

The Residence staff try to make the first family feel as normal as possible. Sometimes that can be as simple as giving them a couple of precious hours to eat dinner together as a family or watch a movie. But the break doesn't last long. As they eat, two binders—one for the president and one for the first lady—are placed on a small table outside the dining room. These binders contain drafts of speeches and work for the evening. The first lady often receives questions from her staff about decisions that need to be made. The president has national security issues to consider. Relaxing is not easy for a president and first lady!

MORE THAN AN EMPLOYEE

Residence staff get to know the first family very well. In some cases, they can even tease and have playful moments with the president and his family.

President George H. W. Bush and First Lady Barbara Bush, who lived in the White House from 1989 to 1993, tried to put everyone around them at ease. Barbara remembered one scene during the Persian Gulf War when she was anxiously watching the news. As she was waiting for her husband to walk in, White House maître d' George Hannie asked her, "What would you like to drink? And what do you think Pops would like?" "Pops" was a nickname from George H. W. Bush's youth. While he was in the White House, no one outside his family used the nickname.

Barbara Bush laughed at the memory. "I said to him— and he knew *I* was joking, and I knew *he* was joking; we were that close—'George, you can't say that about the *president of the United States.*'"

"Trust me, Mrs. Bush," Hannie said, without missing a beat. "At the White House presidents come and go. But George Hannie stays."

"We had that kind of a relationship, where you could tease and laugh," Barbara Bush said. "And yet, when sad things happened to either one of us, we were supportive."

ALL IN A DAY'S WORK

As part of their regular routine, Residence staff often interact with heads of state and leaders from all over the world. It is an amazing part of the job. In 1976, Queen Elizabeth II and Prince Philip of England were guests at the White House, there to celebrate the two hundredth anniversary of the American Revolution. Butler Lynwood Westray remembered going into the Red Room with fellow butler Sam Washington and finding Prince Philip sitting alone late at night.

"Your Majesty, would you care for a cocktail?" Westray asked, presenting a tray of cocktails to the prince.

"I'll take one . . . only if you let me serve it," said Prince Philip, the Duke of Edinburgh.

Westray glanced at Washington, unsure of what to do. "He couldn't believe it," Westray said. "No one had ever asked us that before."

Westray and Washington accepted the invitation and allowed the prince to serve them a drink!

"He wanted to be one of the boys, that's all," Westray said. "I was served by royalty. It blows your mind."

STAY WITH ME

While most Residence staff stay on from one administration to the next, sometimes a president and first lady ask a staff member to remain with the family when they leave the White House. The Obamas grew particularly attached to an usher who had been an Air Force One flight attendant, who continued to work for the family after they left the White House. When their eight years in office came to an end, the Obamas moved into an eight-bedroom mansion a couple of miles from 1600 Pennsylvania Avenue, making them the first presidential family to stay in Washington, D.C., since President Woodrow Wilson, who left office in 1921. (The Obamas stayed in Washington so that their youngest daughter, Sasha, could finish high school.)

KEEPERS OF TRADITION

The Residence staff are experts at their jobs. They know what needs to be done, and they make the first family look good in the process.

"These are not political appointees," Laura Bush said. "These are real professional jobs." The former first lady said she admired the excellent service and knowledge of the staff. "They really know how to serve a beautiful dinner."

The staff has expertise in etiquette and tradition. "We knew that any state dinner in the dining room would be absolutely beautiful," Laura Bush said. "Every effort would be made to make sure the foreign head of state felt at home and that the food would be something they would like and that the flowers would in some way reflect their own countries."

The staff understand how to set an elegant table, but they are also able to help the first family relax during casual times. They see the family dine at formal dinners wearing tuxedos and gowns at night, and they see them the following morning when they eat breakfast in their robes! There is quite a level of comfort between the Residence staff and the president and first lady.

Though the first family may sometimes wish they could forget about the formal rules of the Residence, many of the workers say they take great comfort in it. Most members of the White House staff consider it a privilege to do what they do.

"If you're having a little bit of a bad day with a member of the first family or their staff, you step away from it and you

Head Housekeeper Christine Limerick in the Lincoln Bedroom

look at the house," said former head housekeeper Christine Limerick.

At the end of a long day, she would consider the big picture and feel better about her job. "If I would see the White House lit up at night I'd think, *I actually work inside that building, and I've had the wonderful privilege to do that.* It could set my mind straight, and I could deal with the next day."

STILL TIME FOR FUN

The staff and the families they serve often come to respect and develop real affection for each other. And they know how to have a good time together.

During Lyndon B. Johnson's presidency, Social Secretary Bess Abell remembered having a delightfully silly time when, in 1966, the Johnsons decided to order a new china service. Lady Bird Johnson, who was first lady, worked closely with designers from Tiffany & Co. and the manufacturers Castleton China to create designs that reflected her major project as first lady, which was planting flowers and cleaning up America's polluted roadways and parklands. She was especially effective at reducing the number of billboards along highways. The dinner plates featured an eagle, and the borders of each plate were decorated with different American wildflowers. The dessert plates showcased the state flower of each of the fifty states.

When the china arrived it was breathtaking, except for the

dessert plates. The state flowers were ugly and unsightly—a mess! Abell showed them to Chief Usher J. B. West and it was decided that a set of replacement plates would be ordered and the misprinted ones would need to be destroyed. While chipped and so-called orphaned plates were once sold by the White House to buy new ones, since Theodore Roosevelt was president in the early 1900s, tradition held that broken and mismatched pieces were to be removed from inventory and destroyed. The staff had gotten into the habit of smashing the nicked and broken china and then dumping the shattered pieces into the Potomac River so that they could not be taken and used by collectors and souvenir hunters. This was not good for the environment at all!

This time, Abell, West, and a few others decided to have some fun. They went down to the bomb shelter with the faulty plates. They hung bull's-eyes on the wall with the names—and in some cases caricatures—of their least favorite West Wing staffers and threw the plates at them!

HIGH JINKS IN THE WHITE HOUSE

Chief ushers often become trusted friends with the first lady, in part because they know how to keep a secret. In October 1963, First Lady Jacqueline Kennedy asked Chief Usher J. B. West for a favor. "I've gotten myself into something," she said. "Can you help me get out of it?"

She had a dilemma. She had invited a princess to stay overnight on the second floor, but she and the president decided they wanted some time alone instead. They could not cancel dinner, but they wanted to find a way to avoid hosting her for an overnight stay. "Could you help us cook up something so we can get out of having her as a houseguest?" the first lady asked.

Jackie, her eyes twinkling mischievously, asked West to make it look as though the Queens' and Lincoln Bedrooms—the only two rooms suitable for royalty—were still being redecorated, so that her guest couldn't possibly stay at the White House.

West called a White House carpenter and gave him the

elaborate game plan. "Bring drop cloths up to the Queens' Bedroom and Lincoln Bedroom," West said. "Roll up the rugs and cover the draperies and chandeliers, and all the furniture. Oh yes, and bring a stepladder."

Next, he called the painters and asked for six paint buckets for each room and a few dirty paintbrushes. He staged the room so it looked like a crew had been hard at work. No one involved in the scheme asked any questions.

When the princess arrived, President Kennedy gave her a tour of the White House. When they reached the Queens' Bedroom, the president pointed to the paint cans and drop cloths and said, "This is where you would have spent the night if Jackie hadn't been redecorating again."

The next morning, the first lady called West to thank him. She said that the president almost broke up laughing when he gave the princess her White House tour.

HORSESHOES

The Residence staff—both current and former members—often attend the funerals of the presidents they served. When President George H. W. Bush died in November 2018, members of the White House staff were invited to his funeral at the Washington National Cathedral. Both the president and First Lady Barbara Bush were beloved because of how they treated the Residence staff. At his funeral, these workers were seated among his most senior aides.

Bush loved to play horseshoes, and when he was in the mood, he would call the Usher's Office and ask, "You got anyone to play?" Linsey Little, who worked in the house-keeping department, was one of the regulars, often playing horseshoes with the president several times a month.

President George H. W. Bush set up a horseshoe pit next to the White House's outdoor swimming pool, where he'd play against Residence staffers two or three times a week. Houseman Linsey Little was a frequent competitor.

The president and his son Marvin would head out to the horseshoe pit next to the swimming pool and play with Little and his supervisor when they got off work. They held two tournaments a year, complete with players' families coming to cheer them on. Little had team T-shirts made that read, "Housemen's Pride." Barbara Bush joked that the president approached horseshoe tournaments with the same intensity as a political primary!

"We always beat him, until the end," Little said, laughing. "The last year we were there, he and Marvin won the championship." Sometimes after the competition, Bush would grill hamburgers on the South Lawn and offer them to whoever was hungry.

George H. W. Bush quickly forgave mistakes that would have enraged other presidents. One summer weekend while playing horseshoes, he asked a staffer for some bug spray. The worker sprayed the president from head to toe before realizing that he had accidentally used a container of industrial-strength pesticide!

When the mistake was discovered, the staffer ran to the

doctor, who wasn't too far away. "By the time they got there, the president's face was already red," said Usher Worthington White. Bush needed to be "decontaminated" in the shower.

President Bush understood that it was an innocent mistake. "Okay, okay, okay," President Bush said. "We just want to get back to our horseshoe tournament!" No one was fired.

BOWLING WITH THE PRESIDENT

Bush wasn't the only president who enjoyed playing sports and games with members of the White House staff. President Richard Nixon loved bowling and had a single-lane bowling alley installed in the White House basement under the North Portico.

Chef Frank Ruta remembered the night that pot washer Frankie Blair was cleaning up in the kitchen after the first family finished dinner. President Nixon wandered into the kitchen and began a conversation with Blair about bowling. Nixon and Blair ended up bowling until two o'clock in the morning!

When they wrapped up, Blair turned to the president and said, "There is no way my

President Nixon and kitchen worker Frank Blair doing some late-night bowling

wife is going to believe I was out this late bowling with you."

"Come with me," Nixon said.

The two walked to the Oval Office, where the president wrote a note apologizing to Blair's wife for keeping him out so late!

DO NOT DISTURB

Though the staff sometimes develop friendships with the presidents and first ladies they serve, as we saw with Linsey Little and President George H. W. Bush and Frankie Blair and President Richard Nixon, it is clear who is boss. For the most part, the Residence staff tries to be invisible, and they are expected to ignore what is going on around them. They do what they need to do, then they get out of the way. They are not expected to speak to members of the first family or their guests, unless they are spoken to first. And they must also *never* approach them with personal requests.

As head housekeeper of the White House, Christine Limerick learned the delicate dance the maids must do as they try not to disturb the first family. Maids follow the same code as butlers: they see but they don't see; they hear but they don't hear. One recently retired staffer said that she is in a book club and only three of the twenty members know that she worked in the White House. Whenever anyone asked her where she worked, she told them that she worked for the federal government. "There are too many questions," said Limerick, who is still trying to protect the privacy of the families she worked for. During her time in the job, she remembered several maids who left after a few weeks, either because they were too starstruck to do their job in proximity to the most powerful couple in the world, or because they lacked the necessary discretion.

Joel Jensen knew how important it was to keep his cool around the president and his family. He retired in 2018 after spending more than thirty years working in the White House storeroom, buying supplies for the first family. During his time on the job, he said he always tried to give the family space, even with something as simple as offering a greeting. "I would never ever *ever* say hello first if the president was walking down the hallway," Jensen said. "It is their home. It would be annoying to have people saying hi to you in the hallways all the time. But if he says hi first, it's rude not to say hello back."

This instinct of knowing how to read people is an important part of the job. "You have a balance between serving the family and knowing when you need to get out of their way," Limerick said. "Some of these people might not be the best bed maker in the world, they might not win an award for that, but they knew when the family needed them and when it was time to vacate the premises."

White House painter Cletus Clark took these unspoken rules to heart. "I'm just like a ghost," he said. "You're a fly on the wall: you don't hear nothing, you don't see nothing, and you don't say nothing."

MEET BUTLER JAMES RAMSEY

James Ramsey grew up in Yanceyville, North Carolina, and he kept his Southern accent even after living in Washington, D.C., for decades. He never met his biological father, but his stepfather was a tobacco farmer, and Ramsey spent much of his childhood plowing tobacco fields.

"It was rough," Ramsey said. "I told my dad, 'When I graduate from high school, I got to go. I can't stay here.'"

"How are you going to live?" his father asked.

Ramsey wasn't sure, but he moved to Washington, D.C., without knowing a soul.

He was twenty years old when he arrived in 1961. He had nowhere to stay until he found a sympathetic

James Ramsey standing in front of the half moon window in the West Sitting Hall on the second floor of the White House

gas station owner who let him sleep at the station and wash up in the bathroom. Eventually he found a room for ten dollars a week—that was a lot more money back then, but it was still considered inexpensive for a place to stay. He befriended someone who worked at the glamorous Kennedy-Warren apartment building in northwest Washington. He told his friend that he was a good worker, and his friend got him an interview for a job there. He was hired on the spot.

But he was always aiming higher. Not long after that, he met someone who worked at the White House. Ramsey asked his new friend if he could get him a job there. The first thing this White House staffer asked Ramsey was, "Do you have a [criminal] record?" Something as simple as a speeding ticket could cost him the job. "They're not going to hire you with *any* kind of record," he said.

Ramsey had a clean record.

Ramsey mailed the application and waited. "I passed the White House going to the Kennedy-Warren, oh my God, for two or three years, and I said, 'I wonder how in the world it would be working in that place.'"

Finally, someone from the White House called. When Maître d' Eugene Allen and Chief Usher Rex Scouten met him, they hired him that same day. Ramsey had a dynamic personality and a smile that lit up a room. He became known for his thick white hair too.

Starting as a butler during Jimmy Carter's presidency, Ramsey worked at the White House

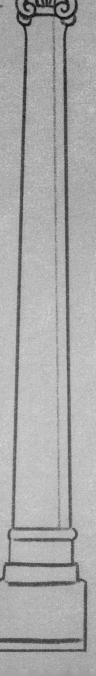

for thirty years, serving six presidents: Jimmy Carter, Ronald Reagan, George H. W. Bush, Bill Clinton, George W. Bush, and Barack Obama. He credits Eugene Allen—"He talked to me like I was his son"—with advising him to keep anything he heard in the Residence to himself. Even decades later, Ramsey would not reveal anything private about those he served.

Ramsey sometimes left his house at five or six o'clock in the morning and didn't return home until two o'clock the following morning, most often on nights when there was a state dinner. Another job requirement for working at the White House: being all right with a schedule that changes almost every day. Ramsey was completely devoted to the job, and he became George W. Bush's favorite butler.

Residence staffers understand the families they serve, no matter how different they are. They would do almost anything for them. "They are the greatest con artists in the world," said Luci Baines Johnson, a daughter of President Lyndon B. Johnson and his wife, Lady Bird. "They make every administration feel they love them best."

Ramsey was single, and he would introduce some of his girlfriends to President George W. Bush at staff holiday parties. He sometimes told

the Bush daughters, who were in college, about his dates. "Jenna, Barbara—I loved them to death," he said. "They were my friends. . . . If they ask, I tell them, 'I got a lady friend. I ain't that old, am I?'"

When Ramsey died in 2014, letters from President Barack Obama and President Bill Clinton were read at the service. Current and former White House butlers served as his pallbearers. First Lady Laura Bush spoke at his funeral, which was attended by dozens of his White House colleagues. She told the congregation that Ramsey did more than pamper presidents. "He made them laugh," she said. "He cheered them up. He brightened their days." On behalf of the entire Bush family, she said, "We thank God that James Ramsey was in our life."

Butler James Ramsey and Houseman Linsey Little in the
Diplomatic Reception Room, December 15, 1992

★ ★ ★

FALLING IN LOVE ON THE JOB

Working in the White House as a member of the permanent Residence staff is more of a lifestyle than a job. Staffers often work long hours and sometimes holidays. They experience situations that they cannot share outside their small group. One woman took a very interesting path to working in the most famous house in the nation.

Executive Housekeeper Christine Limerick worked at the White House for thirty-four years, retiring in 2008. Yet the only hint of her fascinating career in the White House is a Christmas card from the Clintons hanging in the dining room of her home in Delaware.

President Clinton meets Executive Housekeeper Christine Limerick outside the Linen Room on the third floor of the Residence on Inauguration Day, January 20, 1993.

Limerick is very private about her close relationship with some of the most famous families in the world.

She had an unlikely journey to the White House. In 1972, she dropped out of a graduate program in Chinese history at George Washington University in Washington, D.C., to become a waitress at the luxury Mayflower Hotel off Connecticut Avenue, which upset her father. She later joined the hotel's housekeeping training program, but that didn't satisfy her father either.

"I didn't raise my daughter to be a toilet bowl cleaner," he said.

Limerick then got a job at 1600 Pennsylvania Avenue. "When I got the job at the White House, I called him up and I said, 'Your daughter is now the toilet bowl cleaner for the White House. *How do you feel about **that**?*'"

Residence staffers work a lot of hours, and sometimes romantic relationships develop while working at the White House because the staff rarely gets the chance to meet anyone else! In the 1980s, Christine Limerick—formerly Christine Crans—met and married her husband, Robert Limerick, who worked as a White House engineer. They met when she measured him for his uniform!

When she told First Lady Nancy Reagan that

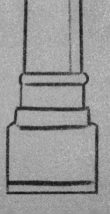

she was engaged, the first lady was thrilled. "I think she was worried I might become a spinster [a derogatory term for an older unmarried woman]," Limerick said, laughing. The housekeeper before her had married the pastry chef, and ever since then, "the joke is that housekeepers come in trying to find a husband." Of course that was not the case. She was happy she met him though. At their small wedding ceremony in Deale, Maryland, about forty of the sixty-five guests were members of the White House staff and their spouses. Working at the White House truly is a family affair.

IN TIMES OF HEARTBREAK: THE KENNEDY ASSASSINATION

While there are many happy times at the White House, there are also mournful times. When President John F. Kennedy was assassinated by Lee Harvey Oswald on November 22, 1963, in Dallas, Texas, it was the first time a president had been murdered since President William McKinley was killed in 1901. It was one of the saddest days ever at the White House, and the staff who had known and loved the Kennedys cried for them. The people who worked inside the White House felt Kennedy's death as if someone in their own family had died. "We lost a friend, a very close friend," Usher Nelson Pierce said. Butlers and maids cried in the hallways.

On the day Kennedy passed away, Doorman Preston Bruce was at home eating lunch when he heard the news that the president had been shot. "To this day I can still feel the shock that ran through my whole body," Bruce wrote in his memoir.

He went to the White House immediately and waited for the first lady, Jackie Kennedy, to arrive from Texas. She finally returned to the White House at 4:00 a.m.

"Bruce, you waited until we came," she said softly. She had become a widow at just thirty-four years old.

"Yes," Bruce said. He told her he would have waited for her as long as necessary.

After a short service in the East Room, he led the first lady and the attorney general, Kennedy's younger brother Robert Kennedy, up to the private residence on the second floor. In that quiet moment in the elevator, standing next to the two people who had been closest to the president, Bruce finally broke down sobbing. The first lady and the president's younger brother joined him. They held each other and cried until the elevator opened and broke the spell.

No one on the staff wanted the first lady to see them cry. They admired how strong she was being and felt that they had to be strong too. If they had to cry and she was near, they would turn their faces toward the wall so she wouldn't see them.

Shortly after the funeral, the first lady gave Bruce the tie her husband had worn on the flight to Dallas. "The president would have wanted you to have this," she told him. (President Kennedy had switched ties just before getting into the motorcade and had the old one in his jacket pocket when he was shot.)

Robert Kennedy then pulled off his gloves and handed them to the man who had served his brother so faithfully. "Keep these gloves," he told Bruce, "and remember always that I wore them to my brother's funeral."

Bruce refused to leave his post to return home until November 26, four days after the assassination. Bruce's devotion to his job—and to the first family—was absolute.

After Kennedy's death, his vice president, Lyndon B. Johnson, was sworn in as the thirty-sixth president. Jackie Kennedy had to move herself and her two children out of the White House while grieving the loss of her husband. She rented a home in Georgetown, less than three miles from the White House, and did what she could to keep life as normal as possible for her children. Caroline finished the semester of kindergarten in the White House—at a school her mother had created for her and her friends—with a driver taking her back and forth every day.

LOYALTY

The staff is there for the first family in good times and in bad, and they are genuinely concerned about the family during those difficult times. The White House staff supported President Richard Nixon and his family during the Watergate investigation, which looked into the president's involvement in criminal activity at the Watergate office complex. The case continued for more than two years during the early 1970s.

By the winter and spring of 1974, Watergate was all anyone was talking about. As each day passed, the president grew more and more exhausted and defeated. His shoulders slouched in sadness as he walked to and from the Oval Office each morning. Electrician Bill Cliber remembered Nixon having a very regimented schedule during his first term, waking up early to head to the Oval Office. But Watergate sent him into a deep depression, and the president's routine "just broke apart."

First Lady Pat Nixon and the Nixons' two daughters seemed to sink into despair during this time as well, and they looked to the Residence staff for comfort. Preston Bruce—who supported the first family during the Kennedy administration—was also there to stand with the Nixons. He remembered the Nixons' daughter Julie tearfully asking, "How can they say such awful things about my father?"

Nixon's other daughter, Tricia, said she always found the staff to be supportive. She said she felt a "positive spirit"—a sense that the staff knew her, knew her father, and loved and admired them as they were. She said that the Residence staff could see "beyond politics." Instead of getting caught up in the news headlines, the staff would make the effort to "see the true person."

Facing almost definite impeachment (a charge of misconduct that likely would have led to his removal from office) President Nixon resigned on August 8, 1974, becoming the first president ever to do so. Preston Bruce recalled seeing President Nixon on his very last day in the White House. "Mr. President, this is a time in my life that I wish had never happened," Bruce told him. In the privacy of the elevator, Bruce recalled that he and the president hugged each other and wept.

"I have in you a true friend," Nixon told Bruce.

TOUGH TO PLEASE

The White House staff does its best to serve the president and first family, even when their demands are unusual—or even unreasonable. One of the presidents who was the hardest to please was Lyndon B. Johnson, who came to the office in the 1960s. He had been President Kennedy's vice president and suddenly became president after Kennedy's assassination. The most important job of any vice president is to take the place of the president if necessary.

President Johnson was incredibly eccentric and he could make people laugh with glee or cry in embarrassment. He stood just shy of six foot four inches tall and had a reputation for looming over his colleagues, an act of physical

"The Johnson Treatment" / President Lyndon B. Johnson with Senator Richard Russell at the White House, December 7, 1963

intimidation so famous that it became known as the "Johnson Treatment."

He began his career as a high school teacher, and he roamed the halls of the White House giving everyone—including his family—letter grades on their performance.

"Sometimes we would have a dinner, and after the dinner was all over and the guests were gone he would come in and he would say, 'Hey, fellas. You all did a good job tonight,'" said Butler Herman Thompson. That night they got an A. Other nights they weren't so lucky.

Johnson was a night owl. He often ate dinner after 10:00 p.m., slept a few hours, and woke up again at 4:00 a.m. The president's daughter Lynda recalled that her father "worked a two-day shift." She said he would get up in the morning and work, then take a break for lunch sometime in the afternoon. "Then he would go to his bedroom, put his pajamas on, and sleep for thirty minutes or an hour," she said. "Then his second day started." It was far from normal, and it was a hard schedule to keep up with.

But the Residence staff adjusted their schedules to suit Johnson's demands. They worked in shifts, with ushers, maids, butlers, and cooks coming in at seven or eight o'clock in the morning and working until four or five o'clock in the afternoon, and another group coming in after lunch and working late into the night or early morning.

Every night, President Johnson received a massage in the

president's living quarters. Usher Nelson Pierce remembered serving on night duty and waiting for word that the president had gone to bed so that he was free to leave. "It was three, four, sometimes even five o'clock in the morning before we'd leave work," Pierce said. All these years later, he was more amused than annoyed.

DON'T LEAVE THE LIGHTS ON

Sometimes Johnson's late-night walks included stops into the basement spaces where the Residence staff worked. Carpenter Isaac Avery was working late one night in the Carpenter's Shop when suddenly the room went black. "Who turned off the light?" Avery yelled. There was a pause.

"*I* did," a deep voice growled from the hallway. President Johnson didn't like lights being left on when they were not in use. He thought they were wasting energy and money.

Avery turned on the light switch and walked out into the hall to investigate. He saw President Johnson standing there next to two Secret Service agents.

"I didn't realize you fellows worked so late," Johnson said.

"I was finishing the frames for all those pictures you sent over," Avery said.

On another occasion, a carpenter was busy when President Johnson caught him working with the lights on—in the daylight.

"He just went after him profusely," Electrician Bill Cliber recalled, shivering at the memory. The Residence staff began to carry flashlights with them so that they would not find themselves in darkness if the lights were turned off!

Chief Electrician Bill Cliber in the Electrical Shop

SPEAKING TRUTH TO POWER

The only person who stood up to President Johnson was Zephyr Wright, the Johnsons' longtime family cook, who they brought with them from Texas. She first realized that she had to "talk up to him" well before he became president.

One night, Johnson came home at about eleven thirty and asked for dinner. This was unusually late, even for Johnson. Wright had gone downstairs to lie on her bed and rest. When he called her to serve him, she forgot to turn off one of the lights before she went back upstairs. When he saw that the downstairs light was still on, he threatened to take the cost of the electricity out of her pay.

She was understandably tired and cranky, and she fired back. "Well, you just do that," she said. "I have always lived at home, where I had to pay my own light bill. Nobody ever told me anything about turning off the lights. But if you would come home on time, you wouldn't have to worry about me turning off the lights, because they wouldn't be on if you'd get here on time."

Her approach worked: "Of course after that he didn't say any more to me."

ONE PRESIDENT'S SHOWER OBSESSION

Plumbing Foreman Howard "Reds" Arrington—who got his nickname because of his bright red hair—was made miserable by President Johnson's eccentric demands. Arrington worked in the White House from 1946 to 1979 and passed

*Plumber Reds Arrington (in foreground) in the Plumbing Shop
in the White House basement, October 27, 1952*

away in 2007, but his wife, Margaret, wrote down many of his stories.

Johnson was never satisfied with the water pressure and temperature of his shower in the White House. No matter what the staff did, the water never came in hard enough or hot enough for Johnson.

Johnson's shower fixation was made clear from the day Chief Usher J. B. West returned from his first day off since President Kennedy's assassination. The Johnsons had just moved into the White House and the new president wanted someone to complain to.

"Mr. West, if you can't get that shower of mine fixed, I'm going to have to move back to the Elms," President Johnson said. The Elms was the Johnsons' Washington, D.C., mansion, and it was equipped with a shower like nothing the staff had ever seen! Water surged out of multiple nozzles with powerful force. Johnson wanted the water pressure at the White House to be just like his shower at home—fire-hose strong!

FUN FACT

Water was piped into the White House when Andrew Jackson was president, in 1833. By 1834, a bathing room was put in the East Wing (bathing rooms were not fancy back then though, and they did not have toilets that flushed). The first permanent bathroom was put in the White House during Franklin Pierce's presidency (1853–1857).

A few minutes after West got into trouble with the president, Lady Bird Johnson asked to speak with him in the small Queens' Sitting Room on the second floor. She was used to her husband's strange and unique personality. "I guess you've been told about the shower," she said.

"Yes, ma'am," said West.

"Remember this: my husband comes first, the girls second, and I will be satisfied with what's left."

A team of engineers studied the plumbing at the Elms, and Arrington went to the Johnsons' ranch in Texas to figure out how they increased the water pressure and water temperature there. When he found out that a new shower would require laying new pipe and putting in a new pump, Johnson demanded that the military pay for it. The project, which cost tens of thousands of dollars, was paid for with funds that were supposed to be earmarked for security.

Arrington worked on the shower for more than five years, the entire time the Johnsons were in office. The water was so hot it regularly set off the fire alarm, but the president said it still wasn't hot enough!

As soon as the Johnsons moved out of the White House, the shower was changed back to normal. President Richard Nixon moved in with his family and took one look at the strange setup and said: "Get rid of this stuff."

CHAPTER 4

Understanding the Past:
Race and the White House

The White House—like the nation it represents—has always had a complicated relationship with race. In 1792, when construction of the executive mansion began, the new capital city was basically a swamp, carved out of the slave states of Maryland and Virginia. At the time, about one-third of Washington, D.C.'s population was black, and most of them were slaves.

African Americans—free and enslaved—helped build much of the nation's capital, including the White House. Many learned to cut and mill the stones used in the pillars and walls of the White House and the U.S. Capitol. These workers were temporarily taken from their "owners" to work at government quarries in Aquia, Virginia, about forty miles south of the capital. They were paid only in food (pork and bread) and drink.

No one knows how many slaves worked on the buildings. Little is known about them beyond a partial list of first names that appear in government records. Slave labor was also used to rebuild the White House after it burned during the War of 1812.

Did You Know?

The nineteen-and-a-half-foot tall bronze Statue of Freedom that sits on top of the Capitol dome was made with the help of Philip Reid, who was enslaved by Clark Mills, who ran the foundry that cast the metal for the statue. The statue had been designed by American sculptor Thomas Crawford.

SLAVES, NOT STAFF

President John Adams and his wife, Abigail—the first occupants of the White House—did not believe in slavery. Instead of relying on slave labor, they hired four people to work for them at the White House. Unfortunately, when President Thomas Jefferson followed them into the house, he brought with him about a dozen servants and slaves. Three of them were white; the rest were enslaved African Americans from Monticello, Jefferson's Virginia home.

Jefferson wasn't the only offender. Six other presidents—James Madison, James Monroe, Andrew Jackson, John Tyler, James Polk, and Zachary Taylor—all used slave labor to run the White House. In most cases, these enslaved people lived in rooms in the basement. President George Washington also enslaved more than three hundred people at his Mount Vernon plantation—he "owned" 123 people, and 153 slaves "belonged" to his wife, Martha, who "inherited" them from her first husband after he died—but Washington never lived in the White House. (In his will, he freed all his slaves, making him the only slaveholding Founding Father to do so.) In 1830, during President Andrew Jackson's administration, the U.S. Census recorded fourteen slaves living on the White House grounds, five of them under ten years old. It was a sad time in our nation's history.

Did You Know?

Sojourner Truth was a former slave who became a famous abolitionist—a person who fought against slavery—and she was also an advocate for women's rights, including women's right to vote, and the right for African Americans to vote. She could not read or write, but she was a powerful speaker who stood six feet tall and had a commanding presence. In 1851, she gave her most famous speech, "Ain't I a Woman?," at a gathering of feminists. She kept fighting for justice before, during, and after the Civil War. On October 29, 1864, she visited Abraham Lincoln in the White House. They were two freedom fighters seeking to make things right.

"In essence, the African American fingerprint has been on the White House since its inception," said Lonnie Bunch, the founding director of the Smithsonian's National Museum of African American History and Culture and a member of the Committee for the Preservation of the White House. Because the country's earliest presidents had to pay

Sojourner Truth and Abraham Lincoln meeting

the Residence workers themselves, they had much less help, or they relied on slave labor. It is a shameful but important part of the nation's history to understand.

While there was a thriving slave trade in Washington, D.C., in the first half of the nineteenth century, there were also many free people of color living in the city. By the time the Civil War started in 1861, census records show that 9,029 free blacks and 1,774 slaves lived in Washington, D.C. In addition to Sojourner Truth, President Lincoln invited abolitionist Frederick Douglass to the White House to discuss using African American troops in support of the Union cause.

WORKING AS STAFF

Most of the more than fifty staffers I interviewed were African American, and many of them said they experienced discrimination outside of the White House during the 1940s, 1950s, and 1960s. Charles Allen, the son of Maître d' Eugene Allen, said that his father experienced more racism at a high-end country club in Bethesda, Maryland, where he shined members' golf shoes, than he ever did at the White House. He was quick to point out that this was not because racism didn't exist at the White House, but it was because no one wanted to get on the bad side of the president.

"People are going to be careful about the way they treat you because of the way these first families feel about these people," Charles said. "You can see yourself sailing out of the gate if you're disrespectful."

Butler Lynwood Westray agreed. The White House "was one place where you didn't have all that foolishness," he said.

Did You Know?

The first African American entertainer believed to have performed at the White House was pianist Thomas Greene Bethune in 1860. He was only eleven years old when he played for President James Buchanan. One music critic said Bethune, who was blind and enslaved, was even more talented than Mozart!

*Westray on the left setting up for dinner with butler Sam Ficklin
in the State Dining Room*

"Even though we were all black butlers, people thought more of us because there we all were meeting kings and queens."

Outside the White House it was often a different matter. Westray told a story about his friend Armstead Barnett, an African American man who lived and worked in the White House when Franklin Delano Roosevelt was president. (Staff do not live there now.)

"One day he caught a cab to go home and he told the driver, 'Take me to 1600 Pennsylvania Avenue.' It was a white cabdriver, and he didn't want to take him. 'There are no blacks living at the White House,' the driver told him. But he finally took him, and when they got to the gate, Armstead got out to go in, everybody knew him; he didn't even have to show his identification." Westray smiled. "When he went in the gate and didn't come out, the cabdriver was still sitting there wondering, 'Where in the heck is that guy going?'"

"I WAKE UP EVERY MORNING IN A HOUSE THAT WAS BUILT BY SLAVES." —FIRST LADY MICHELLE OBAMA

Fast-forward to the 2016 Democratic National Convention in Philadelphia when First Lady Michelle Obama spoke about how remarkable it was to live in the White House as the country's first African American first family, given the history of the house itself.

"That is the story of this country," Michelle Obama said. "The story that has brought me to this stage tonight, the story of generations of people who felt the lash of bondage, the shame of servitude, the sting of segregation, but who kept striving and hoping and doing what needed to be done so that today I wake up every morning in a house that was built by slaves. And I watch my daughters, two beautiful, intelligent, black young women playing with their dogs on the White House lawn."

Michelle Obama had to get used to living in the White House. The master suite in the White House was larger than the entire house she and her older brother, Craig, grew up in. The Residence is very formal and has a painting by the famous French impressionist Claude Monet hanging outside the president's bedroom door. It was very different from the middle-class world both Michelle and Barack Obama had known.

President Obama was moved to see so many African American butlers working at the White House. And many of the butlers had tears in their eyes when they met the country's first African American president and first lady. They did not think they would live to see such a day. Obama said that part of the butlers' warmth to his family was because "they look at Malia and Sasha and they say, 'Well, this looks like my grandbaby, or this looks like my daughter.'" Butler James Jeffries had started working at the White House full-time in the 1950s, when Dwight D. Eisenhower was president. Jeffries said that the Friday after President Obama's 2009 inauguration, Obama "came back into the [second floor] kitchen where we were, walked up beside me, tapped me on the shoulder, and asked me what we were looking at on TV." They talked for a while, and before the president left, Jeffries congratulated him on becoming president, and Obama thanked him.

Then Jeffries said to the president, "I just congratulated you. Tomorrow if I happen to be called to come to work, you can congratulate me for having been working here for fifty years."

Jeffries said that the president told him, "I ain't got to wait until tomorrow. I can do that right now: Congratulations!"

TRUSTED FRIENDS

Doorman Preston Bruce, Butler James Ramsey, and Nanny Mary Prince were all African Americans who endured prejudice outside the White House but forged meaningful friendships with presidents and first ladies inside the Residence. Bruce was the White House doorman from 1953 to 1977, and he was a friend to President John F. Kennedy and President Richard Nixon.

Bruce was a descendant of slaves and the son of a South Carolina sharecropper. Years later, he became an honorary member of the Kennedy family. He watched movies with the Kennedys in the White House theater and looked on as the president played with his children. He watched the president's son, John F. Kennedy Jr., hide under the president's desk in the Oval Office. (Bruce would sometimes have to scoop the rambunctious toddler out from underneath before important meetings.)

President Kennedy shared a special moment with Bruce during the civil rights era. Less than three months before his assassination, Kennedy asked Bruce to join him in the third-floor Solarium (a large family room with many windows so sunlight can stream in) and listen to the throngs of people gathering to hear Martin Luther King Jr.'s historic speech at the Lincoln Memorial. They could hear the crowd singing the civil rights anthem "We Shall Overcome." The president gripped the windowsill so hard that his knuckles turned white.

"Oh, Bruce," Kennedy said as he turned to his friend. "I wish I were out there with them!"

First Lady Jacqueline Kennedy demanded that her children treat Bruce and the other staff with respect. Unlike other first

On their last day in the White House, Jackie Kennedy and John F. Kennedy Jr. say goodbye to Residence workers, including their friend Doorman Preston Bruce, standing to the left of Jackie. "I have in you a true friend," Doorman Preston Bruce said to the first lady.

ladies, she would not allow her children to address the butlers by their last names only. She considered that rude and disrespectful, since they were speaking to older, dignified gentlemen, most of whom had been working in the mansion for decades. "It was 'Mr. Allen,'" said Curator Jim Ketchum, who knew Jackie Kennedy well, referring to how the Kennedy children spoke to Butler Eugene Allen and Bruce. "They called Preston Bruce 'Mr. Bruce.' She was not about to have them say 'Bruce' or 'Allen.'"

PART OF THE FAMILY

Over the years, Preston Bruce developed close bonds with the Kennedys that had nothing to do with race. The meaning of their relationship became clear to Bruce after President Kennedy was assassinated on November 22, 1963, shocking the nation and breaking the hearts of the people who knew and loved him.

Shortly before the president's funeral, Chief Usher J. B. West called Bruce into his office, where President Kennedy's brother Robert was waiting for him. Robert Kennedy told Bruce that the first lady wanted him to walk in the funeral procession to St. Matthew's Cathedral. A car would drive him to the cemetery for the burial.

The funeral service "went by like a dream," Bruce recalled. He remembered seeing John F. Kennedy Jr., just a toddler, salute his father's casket. The great-grandson of slaves, Bruce had never gone to college, so he was astounded to find himself standing feet away from General Charles de Gaulle, then president of France, and Ethiopian emperor Haile Selassie, dressed in their full regalia, at the president's funeral at Arlington National Cemetery. They were just some of the dignitaries from more than one hundred countries who came to Washington to share in the nation's grief. (Sadly, the day was also John F. Kennedy Jr.'s third birthday, and Bruce remembered that that night Jackie had arranged for cake, ice cream, and candles to celebrate.)

For Bruce, Jackie Kennedy had done him the honor of a lifetime: positioning him alongside heads of state and including him among the president's family and closest friends. He was more than a doorman; he was part of their lives, and the color of his skin did not matter.

CHAPTER 5
★ ★ ★

Safety First:
Secrets of the Secret Service

In the early years of the White House, the president and first family roamed the grounds and went into the streets of Washington, D.C., without bodyguards or a security team. Today, approximately thirty-two hundred special agents and thirteen hundred uniformed Secret Service officers watch over the president and vice president and their families, in addition to defending the White House, Treasury Building, and foreign diplomatic missions in Washington. They also keep an eye on top presidential candidates, the president-elect and vice president elect, and visiting heads of state.

Only a small and elite number of the Secret Service agents are assigned to the Presidential Protection Division. These are the highly trained guards who wear black suits and mirrored sunglasses, carry guns, and look very, very serious all the time. (They sometimes wear dark glasses so that they can scan the crowds for suspicious activity without anyone knowing where they are looking.)

When seven-year-old Sasha Obama and ten-year-old Malia Obama moved into the White House, they became so used to the constant presence of their Secret Service agents that they called them the "secret people." First Lady Michelle Obama called them "stone-faced softies" because of how serious they looked on the outside but how much fun they had joking around with the girls behind the scenes.

ON DUTY

The Secret Service was founded in 1865 to stop counterfeiters. The group first took responsibility for defending the president in 1894 after they discovered an assassination plot against President Grover Cleveland when they were investigating a counterfeiting operation. They didn't consider presidential security part of their job description, although four years later they set up a team to watch over President William McKinley during the Spanish-American War.

For the most part, these security missions were part-time and on an as-needed basis. That changed when President

McKinley was shot during a reception in Buffalo, New York, on September 6, 1901. (He eventually died from his wounds eight days later.) In response, in 1902 the Secret Service began to provide full-time protection for the president. Even then, only two agents were assigned to work at the White House full-time.

The Secret Service mission expanded again in 1968 after Democratic presidential candidate Robert Kennedy was assassinated during the campaign. Now, all major presidential and vice presidential candidates receive protection as well.

After the September 11, 2001, terrorist attacks on the World Trade Center in New York City and the Pentagon in Washington, D.C., the Secret Service once again broadened its area of responsibility. The Secret Service now oversees security at major nonpolitical events that could be targets for terrorists, such as the Super Bowl.

Did You Know?

Although Secret Service agents have died in the line of duty, only one—White House police officer Leslie Coffelt—died guarding a president. On November 1, 1950, Coffelt was shot and killed defending President Harry Truman at Blair House in Washington, D.C. Truman was staying there when two armed men tried to sneak into the house and kill the president. Coffelt gave his life to protect Truman.

DEFENDING THE WHITE HOUSE

In addition to the plainclothes Secret Service agents, the United States Secret Service Uniformed Division protects the White House grounds. (These White House police have been part of the Secret Service since 1930.) The agents operate at fixed security posts around the White House, as well as on foot, bicycle, car, and motorcycle patrols.

Although many citizens are unaware, several snipers are posted on the roof of the White House at all times, armed with powerful rifles and other equipment. Agents have been assigned to this duty since 1971. Fortunately, these sharpshooters have never had to fire a single shot in the line of duty!

Having armed guards on watch twenty-four hours a day can be exhausting. The president can never be alone! Presidents and vice presidents can't refuse Secret Service supervision while they are in office. Their security is more important than their privacy. The Nixons were the first former president and first lady to drop their Secret Service protection in 1985. Richard Nixon said he wanted to save the government money, and he hired his own private security team.

SAFETY ON THE ROAD

For security reasons, the president is never allowed to drive. Instead, he travels in a motorcade more than a dozen cars long! These cars aren't for show. They include everything the president might need in case of an emergency, including an ambulance and a personal doctor. The president's car—known as the Beast—even has a store of blood on hand, just in case something happens and the president needs it on the way to the hospital. The Beast weighs seven tons and is so high-tech that it has a ventilation system that could withstand a chemical attack and wheels that cannot be ruptured. An expert Secret Service driver handles the Beast, which can fire off tear gas if under attack.

FUN FACT

In 1975, the Secret Service started the canine program. They use dogs for protection and to search for explosives.

The president also gets top-notch service in the air. Any plane carrying the president is known as Air Force One, although modern presidents have a specific plane designed with special security features. Some have even been designed to withstand a nuclear explosion on the ground! Air Force One is also equipped with a bedroom, a gym, and almost twenty televisions. In addition, the president has access to Marine One, the presidential helicopter, which can fly at speeds of 150 miles per hour.

SECRET SERVICE CODE NAMES

Since Harry Truman was president in the 1940s and 1950s, each president and first lady has been given a Secret Service code name so that no one listening would know who the agents were talking about. Today, messages are encrypted and much safer, but the code names have continued out of a sense of tradition. Traditionally, all family code names start with the same letter, and the president and first lady choose from a list of names beginning with that letter. The names they choose usually have something to do with where they come from, hobbies they enjoy, or their general demeanor. Former presidents and first ladies have Secret Service protection after they leave office, and the code names stay with them for years.

FUN FACT

During a Republican primary debate in 2015, Donald Trump said that if he received Secret Service protection his code name would be "Humble." Instead, when he was actually given Secret Service protection and he was presented with a list of names beginning with the letter "M," Trump picked the name "Mogul."

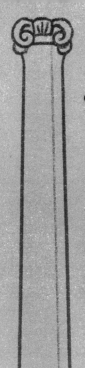

HERE ARE A FEW CODE NAMES OF PRESIDENTS AND FIRST LADIES

John F. Kennedy: Lancer
Jacqueline Kennedy: Lace

Lyndon B. Johnson: Volunteer
Lady Bird Johnson: Victoria

Richard M. Nixon: Searchlight
Patricia Nixon: Starlight

Gerald Ford: Passkey
Betty Ford: Pinafore

Jimmy Carter: Deacon
Rosalynn Carter: Dancer

Ronald Reagan: Rawhide
Nancy Reagan: Rainbow

George H. W. Bush: Timberwolf
Barbara Bush: Tranquility

Bill Clinton: Eagle
Hillary Clinton: Evergreen

George Bush: Trailblazer
Laura Bush: Tempo

Barack Obama: Renegade
Michelle Obama: Renaissance

Donald Trump: Mogul
Melania Trump: Muse

CHAPTER 6

There's No Place Like Home:
Moving Day

On Inauguration Day—the day when the world is watching the president take the oath of office at the West Front of the U.S. Capitol—about a hundred butlers, housekeepers, chefs, and other Residence staffers trade in their vacuums and feather dusters for moving dollies and packing boxes. It is the responsibility of the White House employees to move one first family out of the White House and another one in—and they have less than six hours to do it!

The chore is made even more difficult because they can't use professional movers. It would take too long to have the Secret Service secure background checks on all the movers, so the heavy lifting is left to the permanent Residence staff.

GETTING READY

The key to a smooth move is detailed planning. Everything is done carefully and well in advance. Gary Walters, who served as chief usher from 1986 until 2007, started collecting information on the Republican and Democratic candidates running for president well before their parties chose a candidate. He wanted to know what their favorite foods were and what kind of deodorant and toothpaste they used. No detail was too small.

Knowing the preferences of the first family makes moving day easier. More than two months before Barack Obama's inauguration, Chief Florist Nancy Clarke met with the Obamas' interior decorator to discuss floral arrangements for the private rooms where friends and family would be staying on the night of the inauguration. The more that can be done in advance, the less chaotic the transition will be.

SAYING GOODBYE

The White House belongs to the outgoing family until noon on Inauguration Day, when the new president's term begins. On the morning of the inauguration, the president and first lady host a small coffee reception for the new first family. Just before the first family departs, the Residence staff crams into the elegant State Dining Room to say goodbye to them.

They are often overcome with a range of emotions. They have to say farewell to one boss—who in some cases is also a trusted friend—and they must prepare to welcome a new president and first family. In many instances they have had eight years to grow close to the departing family and have had little if any time to get to know the mansion's new residents. There is rarely a dry eye in the room, even though many may be excited about the future residents.

It is emotional for the president and first family too. On January 20, 1993, when George H. W. Bush was preparing to move out of the White House, he wrote in his diary: "The worst will be saying good-bye to the staff today, but if I lose it, too bad, they've been a part of our lives and they know we care. . . . As I told Bill Clinton, I feel the same sense of wonder and majesty about this office today as I did when I first walked in here."

When it came time to say goodbye, President George H. W. Bush broke down crying, as he had predicted he would, when he saw the staff gathered before him. He couldn't speak.

"We were too choked up with emotion to say what we felt, but I think they knew the affection we had for them all," recalled First Lady Barbara Bush. Before leaving for the Capitol, she raced through the Red and Blue Rooms to hug all the butlers privately. "From then on it was all downhill," she said. "The hard part for me was over."

Eight years later, on Inauguration Day 2001, it was time

for the Clinton family to move out. Head Housekeeper Christine Limerick recalled the mixed emotions that day. "When the Clintons came down and Chelsea [the Clintons' daughter] came with them, they didn't say a word," she said. "I'll get emotional about this now—[President Clinton] looked at every person dead-on in the face and said, 'Thank you.' The whole room just broke up."

During the farewell, Residence workers present the family with a special gift: the American flag that flew over the White House on the day that the president was inaugurated, and the flag that flew on his last full day in office, placed in a beautiful hand-carved box designed by White House carpenters. In 2001, Limerick, Chief Florist Nancy Clarke, and Chief Curator Betty Monkman gave Hillary Clinton a large pillow made from swatches of fabrics that she had selected to decorate different rooms in the house.

THE BIG RUSH

After the goodbyes, the staff gets busy. They don't have much time! For Operations Supervisor Tony Savoy, Inauguration Day is the most important day of his career. The Operations Department usually handles receptions, outdoor events, dinners, and rearranging furniture for the tapings of TV interviews, but on Inauguration Day, Savoy said they are the team that "moves 'em in and moves 'em out."

At around eleven o'clock in the morning, the two first families—incoming and outgoing—leave the White House to go to the Capitol by limousine. Between then and about five o'clock in the afternoon—when the new president and his family return to rest and prepare for the inaugural balls that celebrate the new president's arrival in Washington, D.C.—the staff must complete the job of moving one family out and another family in. In that rare moment, when the eyes of Washington and the world are focused away from the White House and toward the Capitol, the staff is grateful that the public is distracted from all the activity within the Residence walls.

The trucks carrying the new family's belongings are allowed in through one set of gates. The moving job is so large, and so physically demanding, that almost every staff member is called in to help—from pot washers in the kitchen who help arrange furniture to carpenters who can be found placing framed photographs on side tables. Dozens of Residence workers—engineers, electricians, and staff from every department—race to remove furniture from the trucks and place it precisely where the family's interior decorator wants it.

In the six hours between the departure of the first family and the arrival of the newly elected president and his family, the staff has to put in fresh rugs and new mattresses and headboards, remove paintings, and essentially redecorate in the incoming family's preferred style. They unpack the family's boxes, fold their clothes, and place them in their drawers. They even put toothpaste and toothbrushes on bathroom counters. No detail is too small! The staff wants the first family to feel right at home.

THE FIRST DAY

For the Residence staff, Inauguration Day feels like the first day on a new job, without a clear job description or any certainty about what their employer wants. Will the first lady, who has much more direct contact with the staff than the

Setting the Ground Rules

When she came into the White House, Michelle Obama brought her own team of aides from the campaign, many of whom she had known for years. A couple of days after moving in, Obama asked her East Wing staff—the men and women who work for the first lady—and the entire Residence staff to gather in the East Room. Katie McCormick Lelyveld, the first lady's press secretary, remembered her boss making it clear who was in charge.

"This is the team I walked in the door with," the first lady told the longtime Residence staffers as she gestured toward her small cadre of political aides. "You president, find fault with the food, or the flower arrangements, or the way the beds are made?

"There are thousands of things like that running through your mind," said Florist Bob Scanlan, who worked at the White House from 1998 to 2010. "Is she going to call up and say, 'I hate this'?"

Each first family is different. Back in the 1950s, when Dwight D. Eisenhower was president, the White House ran like a military operation. Housekeepers vacuumed after the public tours ended for the day, trying to erase any footprints from the rugs before First Lady Mamie Eisenhower could see them. When a guest walked through the Ground Floor,

guys are part of our new team," she said. She then turned to address her own staffers, including Lelyveld: "It's on *you* to make sure that you know everybody here. They were here before you, and they're the ones that make this place tick. We are on *their* ground now."

The first lady's staff then walked around the room, introducing themselves.

"At the time it was a matter of us investing in them to make sure that we knew what their role was, and how they fit into the bigger picture," Lelyveld said. "*We* were the new kids." This simple act showed respect for the Residence staff and eagerness to work well together.

the houseman would turn the vacuum off and turn his face toward the wall as a sign of respect. But when President Kennedy moved into the White House and saw the workers behaving this way, he asked a staffer, "What's wrong with them?"

In the first days and weeks of a new first family, the Residence staff tries to figure out what they want. Sometimes it's something simple to remind them of home: the Clintons, for instance, preferred fresh bagels for breakfast instead of fancy egg dishes.

But sometimes it takes the first family a while to feel comfortable working with a chef and staff. Executive Pastry Chef Roland Mesnier was not pleased when an aide to President

Did You Know?

The first family can choose from more than five hundred pieces of art in the White House collection, which includes everything from traditional portraits to modern art! They can also borrow items from the Smithsonian museums. In 2015, Michelle Obama opened the Old Family Dining Room to White House tours and redecorated it, adding pieces from contemporary artists. One especially significant addition was a 1966 painting by Alma Thomas, the first African American woman whose art was included in the White House permanent collection.

George W. Bush told him not to worry about making elaborate birthday cakes for the president and instead suggested he make an angel food cake with strawberries.

"I never made an angel food cake with strawberry in the hole!" said Mesnier, a boisterous, plump Frenchman with rosy cheeks and lots of confidence. He knew he could change the president's mind. "After they see what you can do, they forget about what they used to have!"

Roland Mesnier preparing one of his elaborate desserts in the White House Pastry Kitchen, July 16, 2002

Usher Skip Allen talking to Hillary Clinton, February 11, 1998

ON CALL

When the Clintons first moved into the White House, they weren't comfortable having staff serve them. Growing up, neither of the Clintons had household help, and it took them time to get used to never really being alone. To ensure their privacy, they changed the White House phone system so that no one could listen in on their private conversations. This frustrated the ushers, who had a trusted system in place for the purpose of directing calls. When a call came in for a member of the first family, an operator would call the call box in the Usher's Office. "If it was a call for the first lady, we'd put a little key in the first lady's slot and it would ring a bell with her code so she could pick up any phone that was up there close by and the operator would connect her," Residence staffer Skip Allen explained. "That went in during the Carter administration because there were so many people living at the White House at the time that everybody had their own special ring. President Clinton would have just the one ring, the first lady would have two rings, and Chelsea would have three short rings." The staff honored the Clintons' wishes and changed the system.

In addition to handling outside calls, the phones were used to awaken the president at an established hour. Most presidents get up early, by 5:30 or 6:00 a.m., and an usher is on duty as early as five thirty in case the president needs anything. The day after President Clinton's inauguration, the usher who woke him up got quite a surprise. The Clintons didn't get back from the inaugural balls until two o'clock in the morning. When an usher placed his wake-up call for 5:00 a.m., as they had done every day for his predecessor, the president yelled: "Can't a person get some sleep around here?" (President Clinton was a famous night owl, like President Johnson before him. His habits drove the staff crazy: some nights the president didn't go to bed, and the ushers weren't dismissed to go home until two o'clock in the morning!)

GETTING COMFORTABLE

Getting a new family to trust the staff takes time. "Everyone on staff knows when the first family finally trusts them," said former chief usher Gary Walters. For Walters, his favorite moment of a new administration comes the first time the president calls him by his first name.

Other staff members rely on different benchmarks. "The Residence staff knows when the comfortableness gets to the point where we can all collectively say, 'Ahhhhhh,'" Walters said. "It happens usually with the butlers or with the ushers when a conversation is going on and you walk into the room and the conversation doesn't stop. It continues. There's a collective sigh. We know we have proven that we can be trusted."

CHAPTER 7

Dinner Is Served:

Dining at the White House

Imagine sitting down at the table and knowing you can eat *anything* you want—breakfast, lunch, dinner, and midnight snacks too! The presidents and first ladies are under a lot of pressure on the job, but one of the perks of living in the White House is having a staff of chefs—including a pastry chef for desserts—on hand and ready to whip up whatever delicacies the first family requests.

First Lady Michelle Obama really appreciated help with dinner. Her press secretary Katie McCormick Lelyveld said that after two long years on the campaign trail, Michelle Obama did *not* want to think about what to make for dinner.

"There are certain conveniences that just make what are otherwise very long days a lot easier," Lelyveld said, "like someone who's in charge of figuring out your dinner plans."

NO FREE LUNCH

The cook may come with the house, but the groceries don't. Many first families are shocked to discover that they have to pay for their own groceries and personal items, such as toiletries and tissues. First families live rent-free in the White House, but they get an itemized bill every month charging them for what they consume—everything from toilet paper to bananas. They must also pay the expenses anytime a guest visits the White House—if they eat or drink anything, that is—or spends the night.

The first family also pay for their clothes, except for gowns worn to formal events, which are lent by designers and then donated to the National Archives. The Smithsonian's National Museum of American History has more than two dozen gowns worn by first ladies, including Jacqueline Kennedy, Laura Bush, Michelle Obama, and Melania Trump.

The monthly bill, Michelle Obama noted in her memoir, "seemed to add up quickly, especially given the fancy-hotel quality of everything. . . . I had to keep an eye on what got served. When Barack offhandedly remarked that he liked the taste of some exotic fruit at breakfast or the sushi on his dinner plate, the kitchen staff took note and put them into regular rotation on the menu. Only later, inspecting the bill, would we realize that some of these items were being flown in at great expense from overseas."

GROCERY SHOPPING

The first family can't run to the grocery store to pick up what they need, so the White House Residence staff does the shopping instead. Former staffer Joel Jensen, who worked in the White House for more than thirty years, from 1986 until he retired in 2018, used to be in charge of stocking the family kitchen on the second floor. Along with three other people, Jensen worked in the storeroom, located close to the kitchen on the Ground Floor.

The first lady tells the chef what her family needs or wants, and the people working in the stockroom take care of the shopping. "We went to the grocery store every day," Jensen said, although he would not reveal which places he shopped, for security reasons. To reduce the risk of someone trying to harm the first family by tampering with their food, members of the storeroom staff dress in regular clothes and travel to the market in a Secret Service van made to look like a normal SUV, not the big black vans in the White House motorcade.

"If you didn't know who I was and I walked by you in the aisle, you would have no idea what I'm picking up," Jensen said. "Whatever you would buy at home that you need, we pick up because they can't go out."

Jensen appreciated the first ladies who said exactly what they liked. "I loved Nancy Reagan," he said. "She knew what she wanted." *Tell me what you want, and I'll get it for you,* is how all Residence staff think. *Get an assortment of cheese* isn't enough information; *pick up Manchego, Camembert, and triple-cream Brie* is much clearer.

KEEPING EXPENSES DOWN

The first family is not only required to pay their own food and drink expenses, but also those of their personal guests, which can include dozens of friends and family over the inauguration or the holidays. Chief Usher Gary Walters, who worked in the White House when the Reagans and the Bushes were in office, said that "each and every" first lady, except for Barbara Bush, has seemed surprised and not very pleased to discover this.

The bills can add up fast, so many first ladies have asked for menus featuring cheaper cuts of meat to keep down

> ### FUN FACT
> When the president eats meals outside the White House, a member of the military is generally assigned to monitor the kitchen, watch the food being prepared, and taste it to make sure it's safe. Jane Erkenbeck, an assistant to Nancy Reagan, said that when they traveled, her hotel room was always next to the first lady's, in part to make it easier for Mrs. Reagan to get room service meals delivered safely and quickly. Erkenbeck herself would order the food, she recalled, and "it was always delivered to me, it was never delivered to her. Then I would take it into her room."

the enormous monthly costs. The Carters even asked to be served leftovers for their own personal meals!

Jackie Kennedy, who was from a very wealthy family, told the chief usher to "run this place just like you'd run it for the *chintziest* [cheapest] president who ever got elected!" She dropped her voice comically, adding: "We don't have nearly as much money as you read in the papers!" Her husband, President Kennedy, was obsessed with the food bill, talking in great detail with the ushers about how to keep the milk bill down. The Kennedys' social secretary, Nancy Tuckerman, joked that she never saw him sit still for that long or be that interested in anything!

President Obama's aide Reggie Love was twenty-seven years old when he arrived at the White House and remembers the first time Admiral Rochon walked him through the Obamas' monthly bill. "I saw the number and I was like, 'I see the numbers, I see all the things itemized, but for me, a person who's only lived in a household of one with no children, I have no real way to look at that and say, 'You know what, this seems about right.'" But it was a lot, and the Obamas, like other first families, did not want to spend a fortune to live in the White House.

In preparation for the week, the executive chef sends the first lady a list of menus every Sunday. If she sees something she knows her family doesn't like or feels is too extravagant for a family meal, she may ask the chef to look for an alternative, as Michelle Obama did with some of that exotic food flown in for her husband.

Somehow, seeing a line-item breakdown at the end of the month makes the prices seem higher than if the family were going to the grocery store or out to eat. President Ford's daughter, Susan, said that her father would wave the bill and warn her, "You need to be aware that when you have a bunch of friends over I do see this."

Rosalynn Carter vividly remembers her family's first monthly bill: $600 (an amount equal to about $2,600 today). "It doesn't sound like very much, but that was enormous to me back in '76!" She thought the prices were higher than they would be outside the White House because the food has to be examined to make sure it has not been tampered with.

THE COST OF DOING BUSINESS

Former executive chef Walter Scheib remembered that he sometimes got calls from the chief usher, saying that the first lady's office had asked him to keep the cost of ingredients down. Sometimes she would even request that fewer cooks be used in the kitchen.

"Chef, did you really need that many people to produce that event?" Chief Usher Gary Walters would ask him.

"Well, Gary, maybe not. Maybe we could have done it with a couple less people," Chef Scheib would reply. "Let's play this scenario out: We made a mistake at the White House, and we're sitting across the table from Mrs. Bush or Mrs. Clinton, and we're trying to explain why her name is being bandied around by all the late-night comedians. 'But the good news, Mrs. Bush, the good news, Mrs. Clinton, is, we saved five hundred dollars.' How do you think that

Did You Know?

Most presidents and first ladies take full advantage of having a team of personal chefs. Jackie Kennedy knew how a dinner table should be set and how a gourmet meal should taste, but she had no idea how to cook herself. President Kennedy was also hopeless in the kitchen. "The president loved soup before he went to bed, and we have a can opener up there on the second floor—and I think it took him about eight months to learn how to use it," Head Housekeeper Anne Lincoln said. "I don't think [the first lady] knew how to use it either." The butlers would laugh about it with Lincoln the next morning: "Oh, the poor president had trouble with the can opener *again* last night."

Fresh Flowers

The food bills weren't the only costs that worried the Carters, according to Florist Ronn Payne. Jimmy Carter wanted his flowers on the cheap too. Even though the first family doesn't usually pay for flowers, Carter didn't believe the government should pay for elaborate arrangements either.

"We had to go out and pick flowers to do dinners," Payne remembers. "We would go to the city parks to cut flowers." He and other staffers took field trips to Rock Creek Park to pick daffodils and the National Zoo to collect wild flowers. "Police would actually stop us.

discussion's going to go?"

Above all else, he said, "Our goal was to make sure that the first family was never embarrassed." No matter the cost.

Barbara Bush agreed. She had no sympathy for any first lady who is surprised when she receives her family's monthly food bill. Or any bill, for that matter. "If they were shocked, there's something wrong with them," she said sternly.

She pointed out that, while the first family has to pay for food and dry cleaning, they don't have to pay for electricity, air-conditioning, flowers, butlers, plumbers, or gardeners, making their cost of living a relative bargain—especially for a family like the Bushes, who were wealthy and accustomed to having hired help. "I thought it was very cheap to live at

One guy was arrested, and they had to go and get him out of jail for picking daffodils on that big hillside in Rock Creek Park to do a dinner." The White House intervened to get him released, Payne said.

The florists also used other sources. "We'd buy dried flowers from the market, or we'd have our garden-club ladies dry their own garden flowers, and that's what we had to use," Payne said. In other administrations, it was not uncommon to spend $50,000 on flowers for a state dinner, with single arrangements costing several thousand dollars!

the White House!" she said. "I'd like to go back and live there and not have the responsibility."

A NEW PRESIDENT, A NEW MENU

Every time a new family moves into the White House, the chef must adjust the menus and expectations. President George H. W. Bush, for example, *hated* broccoli and banned it from the White House and Air Force One.

Chopping broccoli from the menu was fairly straightforward, but some first families were much more difficult to work with than others. Executive Chef Walter Scheib, who was hired by Hillary Clinton and fired by Laura Bush, said the Clintons were much easier to work with than the Bushes. After serving the Clintons mostly healthy high-end American cuisine, he didn't know what the Bushes expected. Almost overnight, he had to go from preparing layered late-summer vegetables with lemongrass and red curry to serving up Tex-Mex Chex and BLTs.

"It's the only time I ever had a job quit me," Chef Scheib said. "The physical plan was the same, all the pots and pans were the same, the refrigerator was the same, all the ovens were the same, but you didn't know your job anymore. You had to relearn your job literally in an afternoon."

Laura Bush ultimately decided to replace him by promoting the first woman and the first ethnic minority, Cristeta Comerford, who is from the Philippines, to the top job.

While the hiring and firing is at the pleasure of the president and first lady, some chefs stay on from one administration to the next. In fact, Executive Chef Henry Haller served five presidents, working at the White House from 1966 to 1987.

NO GIFTS, PLEASE

In addition to keeping the first family well-fed, the White House chefs also keep them safe. "There is no one more important to the physical safety of the president than the pastry chef and the chef," said former White House executive pastry chef Roland Mesnier. "We were it." There are no food tasters in the kitchen. The cooking staff is responsible for using fresh, safe ingredients and making sure that no one tries to poison any member of the first family.

One way to ensure safety is to avoid accepting gifts of food. Anything sent directly to the White House is either destroyed or sent to a screening facility. Few items make their way to the first family. It's simply too risky to accept packages, even from world leaders.

Former chef Roland Mesnier took advantage of the system only once. In preparing for President Ronald Reagan's 1987 state dinner for Soviet leader Mikhail Gorbachev, Mesnier used raspberries in the elaborate dessert because in Russia raspberries "are so expensive they're like gold, like caviar." Gorbachev must have enjoyed them because a few days after the Soviet premier arrived back home, Mesnier was in the kitchen with another chef when a large brown box from Gorbachev was delivered. He knew that whatever was in the box would have to be destroyed immediately, but first he decided to open it.

Fun Fact

First Lady Hillary Clinton loved Executive Pastry Chef Roland Mesnier's mocha cake. Mesnier made this favorite dessert for her when she was feeling stressed. "I made many, many mocha cakes," he said, chuckling. Sometimes Hillary would call the Pastry Kitchen in the late afternoon. In a small, quiet voice—a far cry from her usual strong, self-confident tone—she would ask, "Roland, can I have a mocha cake tonight?"

And he was thrilled to find two large tins each filled with seven pounds of Russian caviar, a delicacy that can cost thousands of dollars. "I don't care what you do with yours," he told his colleague with a hearty laugh, "but I'm taking mine home. I'm willing to die for that!"

STATE DINNERS

A state dinner is an official dinner hosted by the president in honor of a foreign head of state. During official state dinners the skills of the executive chef and executive pastry chef are on display. While the White House has been home to official presidential dinners since it was built, the first official state dinner was held in 1874 when President Ulysses S. Grant hosted King David Kalakaua of the Sandwich Islands, now known as Hawaii.

State dinners are formal affairs. Men wear tuxedos and women wear ball gowns. Preparation for some dinners can take as much as six months, and they cost an average of $500,000. (Taxpayers cover the bill for state dinners.) Every detail must be perfect!

The Reagans were particularly meticulous about planning their state dinners. First Lady Nancy Reagan went so far as to arrange the serving platters herself. She insisted on vibrantly colored meals; she didn't like to see "gray food" on the plates.

Before each state dinner, the executive chef would plan every course with the first lady. Several weeks before the event, the Reagans would serve the meal to a small group of friends and ask them how they liked each dish. It was a kind of trial dinner, and it was fun for the Reagans and their friends. But it was not always fun for the chef. The first lady would examine the platter and start giving instructions. "'I think the roast beef should go here'—she'd point—'and I think it would look better if the peas were on this side,'" recalled Usher Skip Allen.

If a dinner wasn't exactly the way she wanted, then "watch out," Allen said. He said that she sometimes called the Usher's Office asking to see the chef on the second floor. "If it was really bad, if she was expecting asparagus and got green beans, you had to have a good excuse."

Former pastry chef Mesnier recalled creating one dessert after another to try to find something that would satisfy Nancy Reagan. One incident stands out from the others. With days to go before a Tuesday state dinner in honor of Queen Beatrix and Prince Claus of the Netherlands, in April 1982, Nancy Reagan was seated at a long table in the Solarium, having lunch with the president. After Mrs. Reagan rejected two dessert options, Mesnier presented a third. When she was unhappy, everyone on staff knew the cue: she would cock her head to the right and give a little smile. She

FUN FACT

When the White House was being renovated during the Truman administration, state dinners were held in local hotels.

cocked her head.

"Roland, I'm sorry but that's not going to do again," she said.

"Okay, madam," Mesnier said.

From the other end of the table, President Reagan said, "Honey, leave the chef alone. That's a beautiful dessert. Let's do that, that's beautiful."

"Ronnie, just eat your soup; this is not your concern," she said.

He looked down at his bowl and finished his soup without another word.

Nancy Reagan told Mesnier that she wanted him to make elaborate sugar baskets with three sugar tulips in each basket. He would have to make fifteen baskets for the dinner, each of which would take several hours, along with the tulips, the desserts inside each basket, and cookies to accompany it all.

"Mrs. Reagan, this is very nice and very beautiful, and I really think that would be great, but I only have two days left until the dinner," he said.

She smiled and tilted her head to the right. "Roland," she said, "you have two *days* and two *nights* before the dinner."

The pastry chef had no choice. "You say, 'Thank you, madam, for the wonderful idea.' You click your heels, turn around, and go to work."

He dug in and worked day and night. After the state dinner, when he knew the first lady was happy with the result, he drove home late that night, thrilled. He had met the challenge.

Looking back, Mesnier appreciates the way Nancy Reagan pushed him, however difficult it must have felt at the time. On that long drive home, he recalled, "I thought, *I can make it happen.* This is how you measure a person, when you're trapped like this: How is that person going to make it happen? You do whatever it takes."

Nancy Reagan examines a Christmas arrangement on December 13, 1987, as President Reagan and White House florists Nancy Clarke, third from right, and Ronn Payne, second from right, look on.

FAVORITE FOODS OF SOME OF THE PRESIDENTS

George Washington: Cherries

Thomas Jefferson: Macaroni and cheese

James Madison: Ice cream

John Adams: Fresh fruit

Andrew Jackson: Green beans with bacon

William Henry Harrison: Squirrel stew

Zachary Taylor: Beignets

Abraham Lincoln: Gingerbread cookies

Ulysses S. Grant: Rice pudding

James Garfield: Squirrel soup

Theodore Roosevelt: Steak and gravy, coffee

William Howard Taft: Steak

Woodrow Wilson: Chicken salad

Warren Harding: Chicken potpie

Calvin Coolidge: Corn muffins

Franklin Delano Roosevelt: Grilled cheese

Harry Truman: Fried chicken

Dwight D. Eisenhower: Beef stew, Mamie's Million-Dollar Fudge

John F. Kennedy: New England clam chowder

Lyndon B. Johnson: Texas barbecue

Richard Nixon: Cottage cheese with ketchup

Gerald Ford: Pot roast

Jimmy Carter: Baked grits with cheese

Ronald Reagan: Honey-baked apples, jelly beans

George H. W. Bush: Corn pudding

Bill Clinton: Chicken enchiladas

George W. Bush: Huevos rancheros, peanut-butter-and-honey sandwiches

Barack Obama: Nachos

Donald Trump: Fast food

CHAPTER 8
★ ★ ★

A Unique Role:
America's First Ladies

Few first ladies know what they're in for when they move into the White House. They take on a position with no job description, no role defined by the Constitution, and no pay, leaving each first lady to make the job whatever she wants it to be. That freedom can be both liberating—and frightening. A Texas woman summed it up when she wrote to First Lady Betty Ford and said, "You are constitutionally required to be perfect."

Fortunately, most first ladies have been more than up to the task. Lady Bird Johnson, who served as first lady from 1963 to 1969, said a first lady needs to be a "showman and a salesman, a clotheshorse and a publicity sounding board, with a good heart, and a real interest in the folks" from all over the country, rich and poor.

While the first lady is typically the wife of the president, a number of widowed presidents have had daughters and other family members step in to play the role. As we discussed earlier, one president, James Buchanan, was a bachelor. His niece Harriet Lane served as first lady. Traditionally, first ladies are expected to take up a cause that's deemed weighty enough to be worthy of her time, but not controversial. For example, Michelle Obama had the Let's Move! campaign to highlight healthy eating and combat childhood obesity. The campaign was launched in 2010 when nearly a third of American children were overweight or obese. She helped get a new child-nutrition bill through Congress that year. Michelle Obama also planted an eleven-hundred-square-foot vegetable garden on the White House grounds. The garden—which is still in place—produces about two thousand pounds of produce a year! The Obamas used the food for state dinners and family meals at home, and they donated the rest to local charities. Before the first lady left the White House, she had more than doubled the garden's size to twenty-eight hundred square feet.

In addition to their advocacy, first ladies must spend

FUN FACT
President James Madison planted the first documented presidential vegetable garden. President John Quincy Adams planted the first flower garden.

months planning and serving as hostesses at Christmas parties, Governors' Balls, state dinners, Easter Egg Rolls, and dozens of luncheons and events, all while smiling and looking flawless. No easy feat.

A UNIQUE ROLE

Since no woman has *yet* been elected president or vice president—or even named White House chief of staff (the top member of the president's staff that was created in 1946)—the first lady is the most visible office in the White House held by a woman.

Residence staffers are just as protective of the first ladies as their East Wing staffers are. Within the private quarters, when staffers say that a decision comes from "the second floor," they mean it's coming directly from the first lady. To them, it is more important to make her happy than it is to make the president happy.

Christine Limerick, who came to the White House as head housekeeper in 1979 said, "If the first ladies were happy, I was happy." When she was working upstairs in the Residence and noticed

FUN FACT

First Lady Helen Herron Taft planted the first cherry blossoms in Washington, D.C., in 1912. Today, the National Cherry Blossom Festival is celebrated every spring. First ladies usually serve as the honorary chairs of the festival.

Nancy Reagan casually chatting with one of her close girl-friends, Limerick was relieved. "She'd be on the phone like a teenager," Limerick said. "And when we saw that, we knew she was at peace, everything was good with her."

When Hillary was laughing with her daughter, Chelsea, or Laura Bush's daughters were home from college, the first lady tended to be happy and the Residence staff knew things were all right. So much of life in the White House is anxiety-filled that these lighter moments take on new meaning. "That's when we knew they were as close to having a normal life as possible, and that's what we tried to help them accomplish," said Limerick.

DOING THEIR OWN THING

First ladies share a bond that is less complicated than their husbands' because they themselves were not political rivals. Laura and Barbara Bush, who were part of a Republican dynasty, said that Democrat Lady Bird Johnson—a fellow Texan—was their favorite first lady (outside of the family of course!). The Bushes and the Johnsons have a surprisingly strong relationship, built over years of shared political ambition. Barbara Bush summed up the families' bipartisan friendship in a 1998 letter to Lady Bird: "All Bushes love the Johnsons."

Lady Bird Johnson visited the White House once when

Laura Bush was first lady. Lady Bird was in her nineties and had suffered a stroke. She could no longer speak, and she had to use a wheelchair. When the car she was riding in pulled up to the South Portico of the White House, Doorman Wilson Jerman, who had been maître d' when the Johnsons lived there, greeted her with an affectionate hug. When Laura Bush showed Lady Bird the official portrait of her husband, who she had survived by decades, the former first lady raised her arms lovingly toward his face. So many years had passed since his death, but it was clear how much she still loved him.

NOT ABOVE CRITICISM

First ladies come to realize that even the smallest decisions they make will be criticized. The most controversial thing that Rosalynn Carter, Jimmy Carter's wife, did as first lady was to attend cabinet meetings, something no other first lady had done, at least not to public knowledge. She said she needed to know what was happening so that she could tell the American people.

"I never, of course, liked the criticism, but I didn't pay any attention to it," Rosalynn Carter said. "I had learned that you were going to be criticized for whatever you did, so why not do what you wanted to do."

Other first ladies seem to have taken her advice to heart. Presidents occasionally brought their own china to the White House. Because pieces break and chip (like they did before that fun party Lady Bird Johnson's staff had throwing unappealing plates at bull's-eyes!), first ladies eventually began ordering their own services, even though many people accused them of spending too much money. In the 1980s, Nancy Reagan was criticized for spending $210,000 on a 4,370-piece set of red-and-white Lenox china. Her husband was cutting funding for the school lunch program and other services to the poor at the same time, but she paid for the china with private funds.

Hillary Clinton privately defended Reagan's purchase years later, pointing out that if she hadn't bought it, there would not be a complete set of china to use for large formal dinners. Guests would have to eat off of chipped plates!

After Reagan, first ladies began to order china more regularly so that future administrations could use their china and be reminded of their legacy. Laura Bush ordered a set of 320 place settings shortly before leaving office.

HOME AWAY FROM HOME

First ladies can get attached to living in the White House. It is their home for four to eight years, after all. During the stress of moving out of the White House, first ladies have been seen on the morning of the inauguration stealing a quiet moment to themselves.

"You wonder what must be going through their minds," Limerick said.

Limerick enjoyed walking the halls of the White House alone. "I love the house when it's empty," she said. "It's my favorite time to walk around and listen to the ghosts."

Lady Bird Johnson recalled wandering through the second and third floors in her robe with a cup of coffee early on the morning of Inauguration Day, her final day in the White House. A little more than five years earlier, she and her family had moved into a White House consumed by grief after President Kennedy was assassinated.

She stood in the Yellow Oval Room and the Lincoln Sitting Room, wanting to soak in their rich history one last time. She said a final, private goodbye to the place she and her family had called home for several years.

Late that morning, as President Johnson and President-elect Nixon headed off to the Capitol together, Lady Bird shared a car with Nixon's wife, the new first lady. As she drove away, the last thing Lady Bird saw through her rearview window was Head Butler John Ficklin and Butler Wilson Jerman watching the Johnsons depart. She blew them a kiss goodbye. It must have been bittersweet to know that the next time she returned to her beloved White House, she would be just another guest.

A PRESIDENTIAL FUNERAL

First Lady Jacqueline Kennedy was known for her beauty and style. Women across the country copied her chin-length hairstyle and pillbox hats, and designers made their own versions of her famous suits and gowns. But she is probably best-known for how bravely she handled the death of her husband, President John F. Kennedy.

White House curator Jim Ketchum, who was in charge of preserving and keeping all White House furniture safe and in its place, got a call from Mrs. Kennedy herself, onboard Air Force One, flying back from Dallas on that fateful day. He was amazed that she had thought of calling him, considering all that she was going through. But she was on a mission to make sure that her husband would be honored properly. She asked him to find books describing how the East Room was decorated during President Abraham Lincoln's funeral in 1865. Her husband had greatly admired Lincoln, who had led the nation through the Civil War and who was also assassinated, and she wanted every detail to be the same.

The Residence staff scrambled and worked around the clock to do as she requested, which included covering the State Floor in black fabric and having a riderless black horse in his funeral procession, just as there had been in Lincoln's funeral almost a hundred years earlier.

Like every other Residence staffer, Ketchum would have done anything for Mrs. Kennedy. He spent the next several hours preparing the East Room so that when her husband's casket arrived, it would look just as it had when Lincoln was brought there. It was the least they could do to try to satisfy her requests.

A TOUR OF THE WHITE HOUSE

The tragic way her time in the White House ended should not overshadow the good work Jacqueline Kennedy did as first lady. Her most important contribution was opening the White House to millions of people around the country in a television program. In 1962, she gave the first-ever televised tour of the mansion, which was watched by eighty million people and helped to make her one of the country's most popular first ladies. She won an Emmy Award for the television program! She understood the power of showing children around the country, many of whom she knew would never be able to step inside the White House themselves, what it looked like. She understood it was the "People's House" in a very important way, and even though she came from a family of great wealth, she ended up opening the White House doors to people from every background. Jackie Kennedy herself had been fascinated by the people who lived in the White House before her and her family. She wanted to know everything about the beautiful art and furniture the former first ladies and presidents had left behind. She appreciated history and had a library installed at the White House so that she could devour books whenever she wanted to. And she wanted the first ladies who came after her to have the opportunity to do the same.

When the Kennedys were in the White House, Jackie visited a nearby storage facility used to store White House artifacts not in use. She was very upset to find precious antiques lying on the floor and not well cared for. She set about what she called "restoring" the White House, not "redecorating."

She established the Curator's Office, ensuring that the house's furnishings and artwork would be properly cared for. Now, the priceless furniture that belongs to the White House is held in a computerized, high-tech security facility in suburban Washington. It is organized into categories, with rows of desks and writing tables situated next to chests and rugs that sat in the Oval Office during different administrations. Pieces from particular eras are described and cataloged. The curators know where every candlestick and side table can be found in the massive space. There's even a conservation studio where photography can be done for guidebooks. When a new first family moves into the White House, they can choose from a vast collection of furniture, decorative objects, and paintings in storage.

"All these people come to see the White House, and they see practically nothing that

FUN FACT

In the past, little effort was made to save White House furnishings for posterity. In 1882, twenty-four wagonloads of furnishings from the White House were sold at auction. Some of the items dated back to the administration of James Monroe, who rebuilt the White House after the fire in 1814.

dates back before 1948," Jackie Kennedy said in a September 1, 1961, interview with *Life* magazine. "It would be sacrilege merely to 'redecorate' it—a word I hate. It must be restored—and that has nothing to do with decoration. That is a question of scholarship."

No modern White House resident has transformed the house more than Jacqueline Kennedy, who thought it deserved to be the "most perfect house" in the country. She asked her friend, philanthropist Rachel "Bunny" Mellon, to redesign the Rose Garden and the East Garden, replacing First Lady Mamie Eisenhower's pink with soft white and pale blue. She brought in a top interior decorator at the time, Sister Parish, to help in the restoration, going through the house for "treasures" and getting rid of the "horrors."

"If there's anything I can't stand, it's Victorian mirrors—they're hideous. Off to the dungeons with them," Jackie joked.

She knew the effort would require money and support from wealthy Americans. She asked Henry Francis du Pont, a collector of early American furniture and an heir to a family fortune, to chair the Fine Arts Committee for the White House, which she created within a month of moving in. Members of the committee were responsible for searching for museum-quality pieces around the country and for persuading their owners to donate them to the White House. She also established the White House Historical Association, which publishes the official guidebook and oversees programs. She used the money from the sale of the guidebooks, which were sold to millions of people who visited the White House, to help pay for the restoration. She wanted to make sure that public funds were not used because that was considered controversial, so this was a very smart and creative idea.

Jackie Kennedy did all this, not for herself, but for history. Like every first lady, she knew that she and her family would not be living there for long. She understood the importance of making the capital of the United States as beautiful as any European capital. Just as George Washington had intended.

COUNT THE SILVER

First Lady Jacqueline Kennedy believed that the White House belonged to the people, including those who do not get invited to fancy dinners there. But she became very annoyed when White House guests tried to bring a piece of history home with them by slipping a knife or fork into a pocket or handbag as a souvenir. This happened quite a few times, even at formal state dinners!

The staff would never ask someone directly whether they have taken a piece of china or silverware. They usually shame them into handing it over by playing dumb and asking politely. "When you pick up the plate, you ask for the knife and the fork, and if it's not there, I say, 'Oh, maybe you dropped it,'" said Usher Skip Allen. "We look around on the floor and they usually say, 'Well, here it is!'"

As Jackie Kennedy's wardrobe assistant and then head housekeeper Anne Lincoln said, "stealing" was common because the Kennedys were such a glamorous family, and everyone wanted a souvenir. By the end of one luncheon, she recalled, they were missing fifteen silver teaspoons, two silver knife dishes, and four silver ashtrays. "People come here with the idea that this is their property, so they just help them-selves."

Jackie Kennedy embarked on an extensive White House restoration project. She wanted it to be "the most perfect house" in the country. Here she is with a donated silver pitcher.

She remembered another time when the soft-spoken first lady got aggressive. "One night she saw one of the guests slip a vermeil [gilded silver] knife into his pocket," she said. After dinner, but before the guests had left, she asked Maître d' Charles Ficklin to count the utensils. When Charles reported that a knife was indeed missing, Mrs. Kennedy went right up to the stunned guest and asked for the knife back. He handed it to her without hesitation.

FUN FACT

The chief official White House photographer is appointed by the president to cover his day-to-day activities. The first official photographer was named by President John F. Kennedy. Before that, the photographs were taken by various military photographers. Kennedy understood the importance of photographs and the power they have to shape presidential legacies. He chose Cecil Stoughton, a U.S. Army Signal Corps photographer, to be his official White House photographer.

GETTING BY WITH A LITTLE HELP FROM HER FRIENDS

Though she never publicly crumbled, Watergate took a terrible toll on Richard Nixon's wife, Pat. "Watergate is the only crisis that ever got me down," the first lady told her daughter Julie. "It is just constant."

First ladies have a special bond, and they help each other in times of need. After all, they are the only people who know what it's like to live in the White House and understand the pressures of being first lady. Former first lady Mamie Eisenhower reached out to Pat Nixon in a letter from her home in Gettysburg, Pennsylvania. "Pat Dear," she wrote, "This is not an engraved invitation but I would love to have you come up here when the President goes away—you could rest, walk, read, and gossip with me—know please everything would

be on the QT [meaning the visit would be kept 'quiet']."
She signed the note "Love, Mamie E." She never mentioned
Watergate, but it was clear that she knew Pat needed a place
to escape, and she wanted to be her friend in a time of need.

Everything that happens in the West Wing affects the
president and therefore affects his family. In the months
before her husband's resignation, Pat Nixon spent most of
her time in her pale-yellow bedroom on the second floor of
the Residence, a prisoner of the White House. She would sit
at her desk looking out onto a beautiful view of the National
Mall and answer letters from Americans across the country.
She never wanted anyone who wrote to her to feel forgotten
or ignored, so she tried to answer every single letter.

*Pat Nixon kisses the new first lady, Betty Ford, who will replace her, as she leaves
the White House for the last time after her husband's resignation.*

The Residence staff were very worried when Nixon resigned. They could only imagine how hard it would be on the family. At seven thirty on the morning of August 9, 1974, after he announced his resignation the night before, Nixon was in bare feet and pajamas when Executive Chef Henry Haller found him sitting alone in the upstairs Family Kitchen. He usually ate a light breakfast of cereal, juice, and fresh fruit, but that morning he ordered corned beef hash with a poached egg.

Nixon walked up to Haller and grabbed his hand: "Chef, I have been eating all over the world, your food is the best."

Later that morning, just before walking to the helicopter on the South Lawn and giving his famous V-for-victory salute, Nixon made an emotional farewell speech to his political staff in the East Room. As the staff gathered, Painter Cletus Clark unexpectedly found himself in the middle of the drama. "I was in the East Room painting the stage. I was the only one in there on the Residence staff," he said. "The next thing you know I looked up and all these people started coming into the East Room—I couldn't get out!"

He put his bucket down between his feet and stayed in the room. Standing in his all-white uniform, Clark listened as the thirty-seventh president began his goodbyes by praising the Residence staff, who, as usual, stayed in the shadows and remained out of sight.

"This house has a great heart and that heart comes from

those who serve," President Nixon said. "I was rather sorry they didn't come down; we said goodbye to them upstairs." He remembered how the staff would always smile and help boost his spirits. "I'd always get a lift from them," he said. "I might be a little down, but they always smiled."

The Residence staff took on the familiar role of movers that day, packing up the first family's things and managing as quick a transition as they could under the circumstances.

Barbara Bush remembered being amazed at how quickly the White House was handed over to the Fords. "The day President Nixon resigned, we went down to the White House, we met there for his resignation and Jerry Ford's swearing in hours later," Barbara Bush said. Her husband, George H. W. Bush, was chairman of the Republican National Committee at the time, a position Nixon had asked him to accept. "After we waved goodbye to the Nixons, the pictures on the wall were all of Jerry Ford's family. We were standing at the helicopter waving goodbye while they changed the pictures."

LAURA BUSH AND A GRIEVING NATION

As transitions go, it was relatively easy when George W. Bush and Laura Bush moved in, since they knew the territory better than most. George W. Bush was a frequent visitor to the Residence when his father was president, and Laura Bush knew how things ran in the White House so well that she only brought one chest of drawers and some framed photographs when they moved in. "I knew there was wonderful furniture in the facility where the White House collection is stored and part of the fun of living there was going to the facility and picking out these pieces," she said.

The first lady appreciated the history of the house. "You truly live with the former presidents, you live with their decorating choices, you live with history and chairs that are in the Lincoln Bedroom. . . . It's really a great lesson in history. . . . You are always aware that you're a steward of the White House and that in four years you'll move out, after the election. I think part of knowing that is one of the great experiences of living there, you know it's yours temporarily and that you're the one that takes care of it, along with that staff that takes such beautiful care of it. But you'll move out and some other family will move in."

Laura Bush became a very important first lady because of the circumstances of history. Within her husband's first year in office, she became America's comforter in chief, consoling the nation after the terrorist attacks on September 11, 2001. Inside the White House that day, "the [Secret Service] agents ran in the building and told everyone to run from the White House," Laura Bush recalled. "Everyone who worked for me in the East Wing, and they were mainly young women who expected a very glamorous job at the White House, were told to kick off their high heels and run. And the same for all the butlers, and the ushers, and everyone that was there. They just ran from the building, they didn't really know where to go."

Even after the trauma of 9/11, the fact that none of the staff left their jobs meant a great deal to the Bushes. "We knew we were going to be there [in the White House], and we were confident that we would be safe, but on the other hand they [White House staffers] could have chosen another job or just said, 'You know, this is just too much stress now. I'd rather go on,'" Mrs. Bush said. "And they didn't, none of them did."

Veteran White House reporter Ann Compton says she remembered being at a private lunch with the first lady when Laura Bush told her that she almost burst into tears when her Secret Service agent told her that all the former first families were secure as well.

The enormous tragedy made it more important than ever to have a first lady who could help the nation mourn and offer genuine sympathy, love, and even a personal shoulder to cry on for people who lost their loved ones that day. Laura Bush did a remarkable job keeping the nation together during those dark moments.

She found a new voice after 9/11 and turned her attention to the treatment of women and girls in Afghanistan and other parts of the world. She became the first first lady to deliver the presidential radio address on November 17, 2001, in which she discussed a "worldwide effort to focus on the brutality against women and children by the al-Qaeda terrorist network and the regime it supports in Afghanistan, the Taliban." She was introducing Americans to these terms that have now become familiar, and she was voicing her deep personal moral objection to them and their repression of women. "Women cannot work outside the home, or even leave their homes by themselves," she said. "The plight of women and children in Afghanistan is a matter of deliberate human cruelty, carried out by those who seek to intimidate and control."

A SMOOTH TRANSITION

When it was time to leave office in 2009, the Bushes promised to have the best transition in history. And by all accounts they fulfilled that promise. Michelle Obama's first chief of staff, Jackie Norris, said that she will "never forget the intense camaraderie and loyalty that the first ladies and members of the first ladies' staffs have for each other."

After President Obama's election, Norris sat down in Laura Bush's office with Laura's East Wing team, including Laura's chief of staff, Anita McBride. Michelle's staff was given what amounted to a blueprint, as Laura's staff told them what missteps they had made along the way, which parties and luncheons were important, and which could be safely

Laura Bush sitting with Michelle Obama

skipped. "What they wanted was to completely set aside politics and to help us succeed and to help Michelle Obama succeed as first lady. They were all in this unique position to understand just how hard her role would be."

Michelle Obama holds a unique place as the country's first African American first lady. She had always felt an added burden because of that. "I'd never related to the story of John Quincy Adams the way I did to that of Sojourner Truth, or been moved by Woodrow Wilson the way I was by Harriet Tubman," she wrote. "The struggles of Rosa Parks and Coretta Scott King were more familiar to me than those of Eleanor Roosevelt or Mamie Eisenhower. . . . I wanted to show up in the world in a way that honored who they were." She said that she knew from the very beginning of her eight years as first lady that she would be judged by "a different yardstick. . . . If there was a presumed grace assigned to my white predecessors, I knew it wasn't likely to be the same for me."

In 2017, when she moved out of the White House, Michelle Obama felt liberated from the burden of being a political wife.

Melania Trump has been the most private first lady since Bess Truman, who was first lady in the 1940s and 1950s. Bess always wanted to leave Washington and escape to the quiet of their home in Independence, Missouri. Like Bess, Melania often leaves Washington to go to the Trumps' vacation home in Florida and their luxury apartment in New York City. She has done things her way.

She has spent much of her time working on issues relating to children in her Be Best campaign. Part of that campaign

144

seeks to confront cyberbullying. "Our culture has gotten too mean and too rough," she has said. Her detachment and her independence might help protect her from the blowback that presidents inevitably get. Her husband in particular has stirred strong feelings among his supporters and among those who disagree with his policies. Melania seems to have a habit of self-preservation, which is helpful for any first lady to develop. She is an enigma; it is impossible to know what she really thinks, and that is exactly as she wants it.

CHAPTER 9

First Children:
Growing Up in the White House

There are plenty of perks and privileges for children growing up in the first family—world travel, a private chef, a chauffeur, and a home with a pool, tennis court, and personal bowling alley to name a few. But growing up in the White House, the first children don't have any privacy. *None.* They can never go anywhere without Secret Service protection. And inside the Residence there's always someone looking over their shoulders.

It's hard. Even though they didn't ask for all the extra attention, the president's children are public figures. They're expected to get good grades, act polite, look perfect, and smile for the camera. Even though they're trying to figure out who they are—just like every other kid—they're never supposed to make mistakes, act sassy, or get in trouble. The world is watching! It's a lot of pressure.

BEHAVE YOURSELF

The current generation of White House children are considerably better behaved than some of the kids who have called the White House home before them. President Abraham Lincoln and First Lady Mary Todd Lincoln had two rambunctious children, ten-year-old Willie and seven-year-old Tad, who moved into the White House in 1861, as the Civil War was beginning. The boys earned a reputation for being wild. They staged a circus in the attic and built a rooftop fort. Tad often brought his animals into the house and once drove his pet goats through the East Room of the White House while his mother was entertaining guests!

President Theodore Roosevelt brought four sons into the White House when he was president, from 1901 to 1909, and they gave the Lincoln boys some stiff competition when it came to rowdiness. "I don't think that any family has ever enjoyed the White House more than we have," Roosevelt said. Roosevelt's youngest son, Quentin, had a group of friends

FUN FACT

The youngest son of President Abraham Lincoln, Thomas (Tad), was known for his antics around the White House. Once, Tad discovered how to make all the White House bells ring at the same time!

who the president called the "White House Gang." They threw snowballs off the White House roof and fired spitballs at a painting of President Andrew Jackson. Once, when trying to cheer up his brother, who was home sick in bed, Quentin led his big brother's pony upstairs using the White House elevator!

CAROLINE AND JOHN-JOHN

In 1961, when John F. Kennedy became president, three-year-old Caroline and two-month-old John F. Kennedy Jr. became the youngest children to live in the White House since Theodore Roosevelt's family. The children immediately charmed the White House staff.

First Lady Jacqueline Kennedy was a devoted mother, and family time mattered to her, so she converted two bedrooms into a private kitchen and a dining room so that the family could eat together when they weren't formally entertaining. "If you bungle raising your children," she said, "I don't think whatever else you do well matters very much."

When weather allowed, Caroline's ballet class sometimes

Did You Know?

John F. Kennedy Jr. got the sweet nickname "John-John" when a White House reporter heard President Kennedy call his son's name twice quickly and thought it was a family nickname. It wasn't, but after it appeared in print it stuck with him his whole life.

The Kennedys brought a sense of fun to the Residence.

*Caroline Kennedy in the kindergarten classroom created for her
in the Residence's third floor Solarium*

practiced on the South Lawn, "fluttering like little pink birds
in their pink leotards, tulle tutus, and ballet slippers," recalled
Social Secretary Letitia Baldrige. When Caroline was a bit
older, the Kennedys transformed the Solarium into a classroom, and Jackie invited seven of Caroline's best friends to
attend kindergarten in this unique setting. It was such a suc-
cess that eventually twelve children were in the class four
mornings a week.

The first lady went out of her way to make life as normal
as possible for her children. She took five-year-old Caroline
to the White House kitchen to bake tiny pink cupcakes from
a toy baking set. She asked White House electrician Larry
Bush to put a couple of blocks on the pedals of the tricycle
that Caroline got for Christmas because her legs weren't long
enough to reach them.

A few months later, the first lady asked another favor. "She's grown so much," Jackie Kennedy explained. "Can you please take the blocks off?"

"She was just so in love with those children," Larry Bush said about the first lady. "And she showed it."

Beyond the Call of Duty

One evening, Usher Nelson Pierce, who worked at the White House from 1961 to 1987, heard Nanny Maud Shaw call for a hand from the Family Dining Room on the second floor of the White House. She was feeding toddler John F. Kennedy Jr. his dinner while big sister, Caroline, was on the floor trying to do a somersault. Shaw wanted Pierce to try to teach Caroline while her brother finished eating.

"Mr. Pierce, do somersaults with me!" Caroline begged.

Moments later Pierce and Caroline were perfecting the forward rolls while Shaw and John-John watched!

LUCI AND LYNDA JOHNSON: PROUD TO BE AN AMERICAN

Once the Kennedy children moved out, sixteen-year-old Luci Johnson and nineteen-year-old Lynda Johnson moved in. Unlike most of the families before them, the Johnsons didn't celebrate with grand inaugural balls. They couldn't, because President Kennedy had just been killed. Instead, they moved into a house still in mourning.

Lynda moved into Caroline Kennedy's former room. Luci lived in what was once John F. Kennedy Jr.'s bedroom. Between them was a small room that they converted into a walk-in closet. After Caroline Kennedy's kindergarten ended, the third-floor Solarium became a teenage hideaway, complete with a soda bar, an oversize TV, and two record players.

Not long after moving in, Luci invited a friend to the White House for a sleepover. Luci had a fireplace in her room in the White House, and the girls decided to light a fire. Neither girl knew anything about fireplaces, and the room quickly filled with smoke. Luci tried to put out the fire first with a glass of water and then with a trash can. She climbed on her desk and opened a window to

Fun Fact

President Lyndon B. Johnson named his daughters Luci Baines and Lynda Bird so that they would share his initials: LBJ.

152

let the smoke out. She remembers feeling embarrassed when she saw a White House policeman looking in at her in her nightgown. Once they realized what was happening, the staff ran in to help.

"My mother [Lady Bird Johnson] felt it was very appropriate that I help clean the smoke stains off the walls of my bedroom that first week," Luci Baines Johnson said, still ashamed about the incident decades later.

Luci worked with the maids to scrub down the walls, and they never made her feel embarrassed about the mistake. She appreciated the devotion and support the staff showed to her during her White House years. "The allegiance that the White House domestic staff feels toward the White House and toward the president and his family who occupy it is something that makes you feel very proud to be an American."

THE FORD FAMILY

Gerald Ford had been a Michigan congressman for twenty-five years, and he hoped to one day become Speaker of the House. Instead, through a series of unexpected events, he was sworn in as the nation's thirty-eighth president on August 9, 1974.

The Fords' four children—ranging in age from seventeen to twenty-four years old—found their father's sudden promotion an abrupt and earth-shattering change. For almost twenty years, while their father was in Congress and even while he was vice president, the family had lived in a four-bedroom, two-bathroom brick colonial house on a quarter-acre lot in Alexandria, Virginia, across the Potomac River from the White House. It was a modest upper-middle-class home. When Ford became vice president, their two-car garage became home to his Secret Service detail, and bulletproof glass was installed in their master bedroom.

The Fords had to wait seven days to move into the White House after their father became president because the Nixons needed time to move out. The Nixon family's departure surprised some Residence staff because even though Watergate had dragged on for years, President Nixon's decision to resign came suddenly and his family was not prepared to leave.

Steve Ford was just a couple weeks away from starting his freshman year at Duke University in August 1974 when his father was thrust into the presidency. "All of a sudden we all got Secret Service agents and life changed," Steve Ford said. "Trust me, at eighteen years old, that's not really the group you're hoping to hang out with."

On his first day in the White House, Steve called his best friend, who lived around the corner from him in Alexandria. "You gotta come over," Steve said. "You gotta see this place." He gave his friend a tour and took him up to the Solarium, with its rooftop access. They took out a stereo and blasted the 1971 hit "Stairway to Heaven," recorded by English rock band Led Zeppelin, from the roof of the White House.

"That was my first night in the White House," Steve said. "Eugene, the butler, knew what we did, and I was so thankful that he never ratted me out to my parents. The staff knows everything you do."

Steve appreciated the loyalty of the Residence staff. "The White House really belonged to the staff, because they were the ones who were there for four, five, six different administrations," he said.

Steve Ford remembered his White House years vividly. "It was truly like living in a museum," he said. "Everything dates back to Lincoln or Jefferson. I can remember moving in there—at home usually I put my feet up on the table where we lived in Alexandria—but Mom goes, 'Don't put your feet up there! That's Jefferson's table.'"

Fun Fact

Susan Ford, the youngest of President Ford's four children, convinced her parents to host her senior prom in the East Room of the White House in 1975. It was the first—and only—high school prom ever held there! Susan's classmates raised the money they needed for the prom, which cost $1,200 (more than $5,600 in today's dollars). They held school fairs and bake sales, and Susan and her classmates saved money by putting the floral centerpieces together themselves.

Susan Ford's White House prom

AMY CARTER

Georgia governor Jimmy Carter defeated Gerald Ford in the 1976 election. The Carters had four children, but only nine-year-old Amy would move to the White House with her parents. (Her three older brothers were adults.)

Amy did her best to perform her role as first daughter, but it wasn't always easy. Rosalynn Carter, Amy's mother and the first lady, remembered a time when Amy was supposed to attend a White House reception for a conservation program for children set up by the Department of Energy. Hundreds of children were waiting to see her on the South Lawn, but Amy had her braces tightened that morning and her teeth hurt so much that she was crying. Instead of letting her off the hook, the first lady gave her eye drops so it didn't look like she had been crying, and sent her outside to make her appearance. She had a job to do, like every presidential child.

Amy didn't like

> ### Fun Fact
>
> On the South Lawn of the White House, Amy Carter had a tree house, which had been designed by her father and built by a White House architect. It stood about five feet off the ground and offered Amy a quiet place to read by herself. She loved to read. Caroline Kennedy had a similar hideaway that her father, President Kennedy, had built for her where he could look out at her playing with her kindergarten friends while he worked in the Oval Office.

Amy Carter with her parents, President Jimmy Carter and First Lady Rosalynn Carter

to be recognized when she was out in public. Sometimes, when people spotted her, Amy would pretend that the closest Secret Service agent was her father!

The fame of being a White House kid made it even harder for her to attend a big Washington, D.C., public school. She is the most recent presidential child to attend a public school; the rest since have gone to private school. It was very unusual for a president's child to be going to public school where there were more children and less privacy. And it was difficult for a girl trailed by Secret Service agents to fit in, especially when her teacher kept her indoors during recess to protect her.

While most kids are praised if they love to read, Amy's love of reading sometimes got her in trouble. Reporters were appalled when she brought a book to a state dinner because they thought it was disrespectful to the other invited guests. The first lady explained that Amy had grown up reading at political events, and she was tired of listening to political speeches, so the Carters sometimes let her take a book or coloring book so that she would have something to do. "Being a child growing up with adults," Rosalynn said, "she learned to be just alone in her own little world no matter where she was." Amy even slipped a book in her coat pocket just in case she got bored during her father's inaugural address!

MEET MARY PRINCE: NANNY, BUDDY, EX-CON

In the early 1970s, Mary Prince started caring for Amy Carter when she was three years old and her father was governor of Georgia. Prince was twenty-seven years old and Amy's constant companion. They played hide-and-seek and climbed trees, and later, when the Carters moved into the White House, Prince helped a nine-year-old Amy adjust to her new life.

A year before she started working for the Carters, Mary's life was very different. She was serving a life sentence in prison for killing a man in Lumpkin, Georgia. Prince was chosen for a prison trustee program that assigned prisoners to work at the governor's mansion, doing yardwork, cooking, and caring for the family's children.

"When I first got the call to go to the governor's mansion, I didn't know what to expect," Mary Prince said. "Amy and I, we hit it off the very first day. . . . From that day on, it was me and Amy."

Mary and Amy playing on the South Lawn

First Lady Rosalynn Carter and President Jimmy Carter believed Mary was "totally innocent" of the crime. "She had nothing to do with it," Rosalynn insisted. Prince's troubles began in April 1970 when her cousin got into a fight with a man and another woman outside a bar. According to Prince, she was trying to wrestle the gun away from them when it accidentally went off.

"I was in the wrong place at the wrong time," Prince said. She was not well represented by her court-appointed attorney.

"Hers was a story all too common among the poor and the black before some of the legal reforms were imposed on our nation," President Carter wrote.

When the Carters moved into the White House, Prince was given permission to travel to Washington for the inauguration, even though she was not eligible for parole for another three months. She spent two nights in the White House and went to an inaugural ball wearing a gown she had sewn herself.

Before she left to go back to Georgia, the new first lady asked her, "How would you like to work in this big old place?" One letter from the Carters to the Georgia prison officials, and Mary was free to work as Amy's nanny. Mary moved into a bedroom on the third floor of the White House and was paid $6,000 a year, an amount equal to about $25,000 in today's dollars. An unusual agreement was made for President

Carter to serve as Mary's parole officer while he was in office. Ultimately, after a reexamination of her case, Prince was granted a full pardon.

Mary has mostly happy memories of her time in the White House and she grew very close to Rosalynn Carter. One evening when she was walking by the pool on the south side of the West Wing (President Gerald Ford had an outdoor pool built in 1975 after the indoor pool was closed), she happened upon the first lady doing laps. "Come on in!" Rosalynn shouted. Prince wasn't in a bathing suit. "Just dive in in your uniform!" the first lady said, laughing. Mary kicked off her shoes and jumped into the pool in her starched white nanny uniform and showed the first lady what she had learned in her swimming class. (Amy loved to swim, so Mary started taking lessons herself.) Prince says that evening, "just me and the first lady together out there swimming," is her favorite memory of her time in the White House.

Prince maintained her close relationship with the Carter family. Today, she lives about three blocks away from the Carters in Plains, Georgia. She helps to take care of their grandchildren, and they love her dearly.

CHELSEA CLINTON

Chelsea Clinton was twelve years old when she moved into the White House. The Clintons fiercely guarded her privacy and asked the media to limit their coverage of her at public events. For the most part, journalists respected their wishes.

The Residence staff also protected Chelsea. They wanted her to feel loved. Maid Betty Finney said she was like her own child. "Teenagers, you're thinking rudeness. That was never, ever Chelsea. I had never seen her be rude in the entire stint I had there," Finney said. "She wrote me a note thanking me for my services. That's just the way she was."

The Clintons felt it was important not to allow Chelsea to become spoiled in the White House. Chelsea tried not to ask too much of the staff. In fact, she often told the chef not to worry about cooking for her. Instead, she would make her own dinner: Kraft macaroni and cheese.

Chelsea liked hanging out with her classmates. She once invited friends from her private school, Sidwell Friends, to do a sort of informal internship with the Residence staff. Chelsea and her friends spent part of the day in each department, learning how to cook, clean, and arrange flowers. She proudly showed her parents her flower arrangement—which was displayed in the Red Room—and made them try some of the meals she learned to prepare.

Chelsea was a vegetarian, and her mother wanted to make sure she would be able to prepare healthy food for herself when she went to Stanford University after graduation.

"Mrs. Clinton had decided they wanted Chelsea to be a little bit more self-sufficient and didn't necessarily want her going to the dining hall and out to restaurants each night," Executive Chef Walter Scheib said. "So I got a call from Mrs. Clinton asking if I would teach Chelsea how to cook."

Chef Scheib enjoyed the time he spent with Chelsea. "She was an extremely quick study, and, as everyone knows now, she is very, very bright," he said. Even at seventeen she was well aware of the staff's sacrifice. "She's a very intense person who didn't take this opportunity lightly. She respected us tremendously in terms of us offering her our time."

At the end of their lessons, Chef Scheib gave her a chef's coat inscribed: "Chelsea Clinton, First Daughter." The

White House calligraphers even made her a diploma: "Walter Scheib's White House Cooking School." Later, Chelsea sent Scheib a note: "Thank you very much for letting me take your time. I hope I wasn't too much trouble."

★ ★ ★

KEEP IN TOUCH

Before a new president and his family move into the White House—after the election in November and before the inauguration in January—it is tradition for the new first lady to get a guided tour of the Residence from the departing first lady.

For example, in 2008, after Barack Obama won the presidential election, First Lady Laura Bush invited Michelle Obama to come once for a private visit and then to come back with the Obamas' daughters, Sasha and Malia, for a visit when the Bushes' daughters, Jenna and Barbara, were home.

At the end of President Barack Obama's two terms, the Bush daughters wrote a letter to the Obama daughters recalling their first visit to the White House eight years earlier. They remembered showing Sasha and Malia the bowling alley, the movie theater, and the famous Lincoln Bedroom. They remembered showing the Obamas the best technique for holding on and sliding down a banister outside the third-floor Solarium.

They also encouraged the Obamas to keep in touch with the Residence staff and the Secret Service. "We know it wasn't always easy—the two of you and the two of us were teenagers trailed by men in backpacks—but they put their lives on hold for us," Barbara and Jenna wrote after the Obamas left office.

The Bush daughters understood the stress of living in the spotlight. "You have lived through the unbelievable pressure of the White House," they wrote. "You have listened to harsh criticism of your parents by people who had never even met them. You stood by as your precious parents were reduced to headlines. Your parents, who put you first and who not only showed you but gave you the world. As always, they will be rooting for you as you begin your next chapter. And so will we."

Michelle Obama really appreciated the support her girls got from the other children who had lived in the White House. "I love those girls," Michelle Obama said about Barbara and Jenna Bush and Chelsea Clinton. "I will love them forever for the kind of support they provided to my daughters. . . . If someone went after them in the press, Jenna would get in there and say something and Chelsea would send a tweet out. That made a big, big difference."

JENNA AND BARBARA BUSH

President George W. Bush's twin daughters, Jenna and Barbara—affectionately described as "wild little girls" by their grandmother when they were younger—were already familiar with the White House when their father was elected. They had spent a lot of time at the Residence when their grandparents George H. W. Bush and Barbara Bush lived there.

The Bush girls attended their grandfather's inauguration on January 20, 1989. They were seven years old and asked their parents if they could go inside to get out of the freezing cold. "We let them go in, even though the White House probably was not ready for new members of the next family to come in!" Laura Bush said. "The girls came in and [Head Florist] Nancy Clarke met them at the door and asked them if they wanted to go to the Flower Shop and make a little bouquet for their bedroom. They never forgot it. They went downstairs to the shop and made little flower arrangements to bring up to us when we came in from the parade."

Years later, when their father told them he was running for president in 2000, the eighteen-year-olds tried to convince him not to. They knew all too well the stresses of the job. They also knew there would always be constraints and limits that come with life in that particular bubble.

"It's a miserable life for a teenager," said Usher Nelson Pierce. "It was very difficult to be confined, knowing that you couldn't do anything without [the Secret Service] right on your tail."

*Obama girls being shown how to slide down
a banister by the Bush daughters*

SASHA AND MALIA OBAMA

Like other children of politicians, Sasha and Malia Obama spent a lot of time on the campaign trail. While on the road, they often played cards with the young campaign staff, and they always kept an eye out for a nearby ice cream store. During the 2008 presidential campaign, their father was traveling so much that they did not see him often, so their mother made a special effort to come home from a busy day of campaigning in time to tuck her kids in at night. On a good day she could get home in time to have dinner with her daughters.

Sasha and Malia had one request of their parents during the grueling campaign: at the end of it all, they wanted a dog. Three months after moving into the White House they got their wish when Senator Ted Kennedy gave the girls a six-month-old Portuguese water dog named Bo. Sasha and Malia spent hours running around on the South Lawn with Bo.

Early in President Obama's second term, the Obamas added another puppy of the same breed named Sunny. The Obamas asked the press to leave the girls alone, but they did agree to periodic press encounters with Bo and Sunny.

The Obamas did all they could to keep life normal for their girls. Like other parents on work trips, President Obama would bring back souvenirs for his daughters from his many trips around the world: globes for Sasha and key chains for Malia. Still, Michelle Obama felt guilty at times: "You want your kids to grow up normal. You want them to be able to have wonderful experiences privately. And you want them to be able to fail and stumble privately, like any other kids," the first lady said. "When they're not allowed to do that, it's unfair, and you feel guilty about it. Because they didn't choose this life."

Malia took driving lessons with the Secret Service, and Sasha took swim lessons at American University, not far from the White House. On Monday and Wednesday nights, her famous mom would slip in, often unnoticed, to watch her daughter at swim practice. When Malia played tennis in high school, Michelle stayed behind in a Secret Service van, watching her matches from a window, worried about causing a scene if she sat courtside.

It is easy to become spoiled when your parents are so famous that you get a birthday serenade from Janelle Monáe and Kendrick Lamar (which happened to Malia in 2016). But the Obamas worked hard to make sure there was some discipline: the girls had to make their own beds and got dessert only on weekends. (That rule was broken when their grandmother—Michelle Obama's mother, Marian Robinson—was in charge. She let the girls eat ice cream and popcorn any day of the week.)

Did You Know?

Marian Robinson, Michelle Obama's mother, lived on the third floor of the White House, but went out of her way to give the family privacy. "I'm going home," Robinson would say before dinner as she walked upstairs to her private suite, giving her daughter time alone with her husband and children. Florist Bob Scanlan put fresh flowers in Robinson's living room and bedroom. When Scanlan came in to replace a floral arrangement, she would often tell him not to bother. "That's fine, but the other flowers still look good to me," she'd say. Marian even insisted on doing her own laundry!

On election night in 2008, Barack Obama made a victory speech when he won the presidency at Chicago's Grant Park and a whopping 200,000 people showed up to hear him speak. On the way there, the Obama family had a police-escorted motorcade along Lake Shore Drive, which the Secret Service cleared portions of so that president-elect Obama could get there quickly.

"Daddy," their ten-year-old daughter, Malia, said from the back seat of the big SUV, "there's no one on the road, I don't think anyone's coming to your celebration."

Barack and Michelle Obama looked at each other and smiled.

The first lady made a point to try to have the girls learn what they could while they were in the White House. She asked the florists to label all the flowers in the arrangements in their living quarters so that she and her daughters could learn the different names. She also asked Butler Smile "Smiley" Saint-Aubin, who was from Haiti and spoke French, to speak in his native tongue when serving her daughters so that they could start learning the language.

Florist Bob Scanlan wanted the Obamas to have a special

first Christmas season at the White House, so he made box-wood Christmas trees and put one on Malia's dresser and one on Sasha's mantel. Malia especially liked hers. When Scanlan went into her room to check on the tree he found a sticky note waiting for him: "Florist: I really like my tree. If it's not too much to ask could I please have lights on it? If not, I understand." She signed it with a heart.

Scanlan took the note off the dresser and brought it down to the Flower Shop. "Now you tell me, how could I *not* put lights on that tree?" he asked.

BARRON TRUMP

The Residence staff was delighted when they learned that ten-year-old Barron Trump would become the first young boy to live in the White House since John F. Kennedy Jr. in the 1960s. But they had to wait to welcome their new resident. To make Barron's transition to the White House easier, his mother, First Lady Melania Trump, waited five months to move from New York City to Washington, D.C., so that Barron could finish fourth grade. It was an unprecedented decision: no other first lady had delayed the move before, and the staff was eager and anxious for them to move in.

FUN FACT
Barron Trump is fluent in English and Slovenian.

The Residence staff put up soccer nets on the South Lawn for Barron. According to Head Engineer Brian Rock, who retired in 2017, Barron wanted a behind-the-scenes tour of the chill room (where the giant air-conditioning and heating units for the home are kept). The staff was more than happy to show him around.

From those private tours to cooking classes, to somersault lessons, the staff would do almost anything to support the presidents' children.

CHAPTER 10
★ ★ ★

Lions and Tigers and Bears, Oh My!:
Pets in the White House

Wouldn't it be fun to have your very own pony? How about a parrot, a raccoon, or even a pygmy hippo? While there is a lot of responsibility that first children bear, one of the upsides of being a kid in the White House is having as many pets as your parents will allow—along with a group of dedicated White House staff to help take care of them.

Over the years, a number of strange animals have lived at the White House. President Thomas Jefferson befriended two grizzly bears, given to him by American explorer Captain Zebulon Pike. Of course he didn't allow the grizzlies to roam the White House grounds—the animals lived in a cage on the front lawn for several months—but Jefferson also had four pet mockingbirds, which he did allow to fly freely inside the White House!

President Calvin Coolidge welcomed a number of animals into the White House, including dogs, a bear, raccoons, birds, a goose, a donkey, two lion cubs, a wallaby—an animal similar to a kangaroo—as well as a bobcat named Smoky and a pygmy hippo named Billy! One of the raccoons was named Rebecca, and First Lady Grace Coolidge would put her on a leash and walk her like a dog on the South Lawn.

A GIFT FOR YOU

Some of the animals were gifts from foreign dignitaries. President Martin Van Buren was given two tiger cubs by the sultan of Omar in 1837. (They were donated to the National Zoo in Washington, D.C.)

John Quincy Adams was given an alligator by the French general Marquis de Lafayette. And that wasn't the only White House alligator! Herbert Hoover's son kept several alligators as pets, occasionally allowing them to wander around on the White House lawn.

In 1959, President Eisenhower received a 440-pound baby forest elephant, Dzimbo, from the French territories in West Africa. After stopping by the White House, Dzimbo took up residence at the National Zoo.

INDOOR AND OUTDOOR ANIMALS

From the earliest days, animals have lived at the White House. At first, most of the animals were working horses and cows kept for milk. President William Howard Taft—who moved to the White House in 1909—was the first president to travel by car instead of carriage. He was also the last to keep a cow on the grounds because dairy companies began to deliver milk.

While it may seem obvious that some animals belong in the barn and others can come inside the house, sometimes the boundaries between indoor and outdoor animals got a bit fuzzy. Tad Lincoln, one of President Abraham Lincoln and Mary Todd Lincoln's rambunctious sons, who we talked about before, brought his pony and pet goat inside to sleep by his side at night when he was seven years old. Who is going to say no to the child of a president?

This wasn't the only pony to tour the interior of the White House either. The rowdy children of President Theodore Roosevelt had an impressive array of pets, including a macaw named Eli Yale, dogs, cats, snakes, birds, a one-legged rooster, and a pony named Algonquin, who famously rode the White House elevator!

Not all of the unusual pets were large. Theodore Roosevelt allowed his daughter Alice to keep a pet snake. She named it Emily Spinach (because it was green) and she sometimes took it to parties in her purse.

Caroline Kennedy kept pet hamsters. Every once in a while, one of them slipped away, and the chief usher would scurry through the house looking for the runaway. Caroline wasn't the only one with a love of rodents. President Andrew Johnson once discovered a family of mice living in his bedroom. Rather than calling for an exterminator, he adopted them as pets and began leaving water and snacks by the fireplace at night.

UNCONDITIONAL LOVE

Pets may be popular in the White House because many animals offer unconditional love in a town that can be very tough. Harry Truman famously said, "If you want a friend in Washington, get a dog." They also make it easier for the public to relate to the first family. White House pets often become media stars, and many children write letters to the White House pets.

Some animals play an important role in the president's life. President Warren Harding brought his dog, Laddie Boy, an Airedale terrier, into cabinet meetings. President Franklin Roosevelt

FUN FACT

The White House has also been the scene of pet funerals. The Eisenhowers held a Rose Garden funeral for their canary named Pete.

brought his black Scottish terrier, Fala, to press conferences and meetings. When the president died, Fala walked beside his remains in the funeral.

The first ladies also get attached to their animals. First Lady Dolley Madison had a macaw parrot named Polly who perched on the first lady's shoulder as she went through her day. When the White House was attacked during the War of 1812, the first lady famously rushed through the White House and saved an important portrait of George Washington by the artist Gilbert Stuart. She did this with the help of Paul Jennings, who we talked about earlier. What is less well-known is that she also saved Polly before fleeing the house.

WHO LET THE DOGS OUT?

The president and first family don't always have the time to care for the animals in the White House. Fortunately, they get help. Since the 1930s, a Residence staffer has been assigned to care for the pets.

White House carpenter Milton Frame took care of President John F. Kennedy's dogs early in his administration. He was working when Soviet leader Nikita Khrushchev gave the Kennedys Pushinka, a puppy from the first dog to orbit in space. Frame's favorite memory is of a young President Kennedy having a bit of fun on the White House grounds.

One morning, Frame was walking Pushinka and one of

the Kennedys' other dogs, Charlie, a Welsh terrier.

"Charlie, go get you a duck!" Kennedy shouted out.

"And don't you know that dog went straight to that fountain and grabbed a duck!" Frame said, laughing. He had the duck by the wing, and Frame had to wrestle it away. "The president was laughing the whole time!"

Pushinka had a litter of puppies with Charlie. So many people wanted the puppies that First Lady Jackie Kennedy held an essay contest for children around the country, promising one of the puppies as the first prize.

The Kennedys had other pets too. When Johnson was Kennedy's vice president, he gave Kennedy's daughter, Caroline, a pony named Macaroni that pulled Jackie and her children on a sleigh on the South Lawn in the snow.

Traphes Bryant worked as a White House electrician, but he also cared for the Kennedys' dogs. In addition to letting the dogs out and keeping them fed, Bryant trained the presidential dogs to greet their owners on the South Lawn when they returned from a trip on the marine helicopter. President Kennedy thoroughly enjoyed the tradition. He always gave a broad smile and greeted the waiting dogs "as if they were his distinguished hosts."

Bryant was worried that he would not get along with Lyndon B. Johnson when Johnson took over the presidency after Kennedy's assassination. When the Johnson family moved in, their daughter Luci brought their beagles, Him and Her, in her convertible. Johnson was a dog lover, but he caused lots of controversy when he lifted Him by his ears in front of a group of reporters in 1964. From then on he was in the doghouse with animal lovers who thought he was hurting Him.

MILLIE'S BOOK

First Lady Barbara Bush loved her dog Millie so much that she wrote a book about her. *Millie's Book: As Dictated to Barbara Bush* was a national bestseller told through the eyes of their adorable English springer spaniel.

Millie was a troublemaker. While she lived at the White House, she killed four squirrels, three rats, and a pigeon. President Ronald Reagan loved to feed nuts to the squirrels on the South Lawn. When then vice president George H. W. Bush found out about Reagan's soft spot for squirrels, he panicked. "Oh, gosh," Bush told the president, "Millie kills squirrels!"

41st President George H. W. Bush and
First Lady Barbara Bush with their dog Millie

On Reagan's last day as president, before Bush took office, Reagan asked his vice president to step outside of the Oval Office. There Bush saw a sign hung low so that the squirrels could see it. It read: *Beware of Dog!*

When the Bush family was out of town, the White House engineers watched the dogs in the basement during the overnight hours. Once, Barbara Bush returned home from a trip and she went downstairs to visit the puppies. She saw a message she wasn't meant to see; one of the engineers had left a note for his colleague using inappropriate language to remind him to wash the dogs. The engineers were embarrassed that she saw the sign. Graciously, she said, "You are so nice, they are very dirty dogs."

The Bushes loved their dogs more than most. "One of the ways I really relaxed when I was president was walking with my dog," President George H. W. Bush said about his springer spaniel Ranger, Millie's puppy. (Ranger was named after the Texas Rangers baseball team, which George W. Bush had an ownership stake in before he became governor of Texas.) "I bonded with my dog. It didn't matter, rain or shine, he was at my side or sleeping on our bed. . . . He was my friend and companion."

President Bush had a dog treat dispenser in the shape of a gumball machine installed at Camp David, the president's retreat in Maryland. But the White House staff loved giving Ranger treats so much that Bush had to send out a note asking them to stop because the dog was gaining too much weight.

CATS AND DOGS

Some presidents enter the White House as cat people and turn into dog people. The Fords, Carters, and Clintons all came to the White House with just a cat but eventually got a dog. There is something intriguing about the

FUN FACT

Amy Carter, President Jimmy Carter and Rosalynn Carter's daughter, came up with a very creative pet name. She named her Siamese cat Misty Malarky Ying Yang.

fun-loving image of a dog running on the South Lawn with the president that just was not the same with a cat lounging in the Residence.

Even though President Clinton was allergic to cats, the family had a cat named Socks. While they were in the White House, the Clintons adopted Buddy, a chocolate Labrador retriever. Hillary Clinton wrote a book, *Dear Socks, Dear Buddy: Kids' Letters to the First Pets*. (Clinton gave Socks to his assistant Betty Currie when they left office.)

PET PEOPLE

First Lady Laura Bush said she remembered how moved she was by the Residence staff and their devotion to the White House pets. "Harold Hancock was one of the doormen who we loved," she said. "I have a wonderful photograph of him standing at the door waiting for the president to come back with Spot, our dog. They were always great to all the animals. They acted like they were really wild about all the animals, whether they were or not."

Chief Gardener Dale Haney took care of the Obamas' dogs and before that the Bush family pets, two Scottish terriers named Barney and Miss Beazley. "He was Barney and Miss Beazley's best friend," Laura Bush said. "They were in the White House garden with Dale every day."

When the Bushes left office, Haney had to take a week

off because he missed them so much—and, also, he missed their dogs.

Did You Know?

Dogs at the White House are not only pets. Some of them are working hard! The Secret Service has used specially trained dogs to protect the president and his family since 1975. They are tough-as-nails pooches trained to recognize smells associated with explosives. Most are a breed called Belgian Malinois, not German shepherds, which is what most people think they are. They are fiercely protective and also very loving with their Secret Service handlers, who they work with every day as a team.

★ ★ ★

MODERN PRESIDENTS
AND THEIR DOGS

John F. Kennedy:

Gaullie (a French poodle)

Charlie (a Welsh terrier)

Wolf (an Irish wolfhound)

Clipper (a German shepherd)

Moe (a Doberman pinscher)

Pushinka (mixed breed)

Shannon (a cocker spaniel)

Lyndon B. Johnson:

Yuki (mixed breed)

Blanco (a collie)

Him, Her, Edgar, and Freckles (all beagles)

Richard Nixon:

Vicky (a poodle)

Pasha (a terrier)

King Timahoe (an Irish setter)

Checkers (a cocker spaniel)

Gerald Ford:

Liberty (a golden retriever)

Lucky (mixed breed)

Misty (a golden retriever)

Jimmy Carter:

Grits (a border collie mix)

Lewis Brown (an Afghan hound)

Ronald Reagan:

Lucky (a Bouvier des Flandres)

Rex (a Cavalier King Charles spaniel)

Victory (a golden retriever)

Peggy (an Irish setter)

Taca (a Siberian husky)

Fuzzy (a Belgian sheepdog)

George H. W. Bush:

Millie (an English springer spaniel)

Ranger (one of Millie's puppies)

Bill Clinton:

Buddy (a chocolate Labrador retriever)

George W. Bush:

Miss Beazley and Barney (Scottish terriers)

Spot (an English springer spaniel)

Barack Obama:

Bo and Sunny (both Portuguese water dogs)

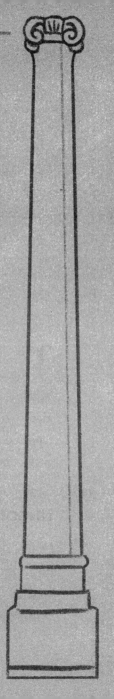

CHAPTER 11

★ ★ ★

Things That Go Bump in the Night:
White House Ghosts

The White House has been around for more than two hundred years, so it doesn't come as a surprise that the Residence has picked up a few ghosts along the way. Presidents, first ladies, White House staff, and guests all have reported hearing unusual noises, feeling eerie spiritual presences, and seeing ghosts in the halls of the famous Residence.

LINCOLN'S GHOST

One of the most famous White House ghosts is that of President Lincoln, who was assassinated just as the Civil War was ending. Grace Coolidge, who was first lady in the 1920s, decades after Lincoln was killed, was the first person to report that she had seen Lincoln's ghost, standing in the Oval Office, looking out a window in the direction of the Potomac to the Civil War battlefields beyond.

Since then, Lincoln's ghost has appeared for a number of White House visitors. In 1942, Queen Wilhelmina of the Netherlands heard a knock on her door. When she answered it, she saw the ghost of Lincoln, wearing his iconic top hat—and she fainted on the spot!

During World War II, British prime minister Winston Churchill claimed he saw Lincoln's ghost appear next to the fireplace when he stayed in the Lincoln Bedroom. Churchill addressed the president, who then disappeared.

While she did not see his ghost, Lady Bird Johnson said that she felt Lincoln's presence in the room while she was watching a TV show about him.

White House florist Wendy Elsasser said that pets could often sense Lincoln's ghost. "Nancy Reagan's dog Rex would bark outside the Lincoln Bedroom like there was a ghost in there," Elsasser said. "They'd shut the door, and he'd still bark outside."

White House maid Betty Finney insisted that the rumors about President Lincoln's ghost haunting the White House are true. She said she saw the famous former president sitting in a chair outside the Treaty Room. "He was sitting there with his legs crossed, he had a charcoal-gray pinstripe suit on," she said. "I saw his beard, his face, the mole on his face."

Maid Betty Finney in room 327 of the Residence

When she saw the ghost, she was so scared that she said to herself: *Legs, let's go, why are you not moving?* Lincoln just sat there, she said, "Looking straight ahead. No expression at all."

OTHER SIGHTINGS

President Lincoln isn't the only ghost reported as haunting the White House.

Some people claim to have seen the ghost of Abigail Adams hanging her laundry in the East Room. Wearing a cap and a lace shawl, the first lady has been seen carrying a basket of laundry to the room where she once hung her wet clothes to dry when she lived in the White House. Some have even reported the scent of wet laundry and lavender in the room after seeing her ghost.

President Andrew Jackson is said to haunt the Queens' Bedroom, the room where he slept when he lived in the White House. First Lady Mary Todd Lincoln said that she sometimes heard the ghost of President Jackson stomping through the halls.

The first president to die in office was William Henry Harrison. He died after only thirty-two days as president. It has been reported he walks along the halls he paced for a short time when he was alive. Others say they have seen him rummaging in the attic.

While he didn't report any specific ghost sightings, President Harry Truman wrote letters to his wife about hearing ghosts in his study. "I sit here in this old house and work on

Did You Know?

President Abraham Lincoln's wife, Mary Todd Lincoln, held séances in the White House, hoping to be able to communicate with her son Willie, who died from a sudden illness when he was eleven years old. In April 1863, Lincoln joined in a séance in the Red Room of the White House, along with the first lady, two cabinet secretaries, a spiritual medium, and a reporter from the *Boston Gazette.*

foreign affairs, read reports, and work on speeches—all the while listening to the ghosts walk up and down the hallway and even right here in the study," he wrote. "The floors pop and the drapes move back and forth."

Other ghosts seem to occupy specific rooms or places in the White House. While in the Yellow Oval Room, aides to President Franklin Delano Roosevelt and President William Howard Taft both reported hearing a voice say, "I'm Mr. Burns." Neither could find anyone speaking. David Burns owned part of the farmland where the White House was built.

First Lady Dolley Madison has been said to watch over the Rose Garden. Some have said that she even haunted the gardeners who had planned to dig up her original rosebushes!

President John Tyler has reportedly been spotted in the Blue Room, proposing to his second wife, Julia.

Some of the White House ghosts seem to come and go. Lynda Johnson, daughter of President Lyndon B. Johnson, claimed that she was visited by the ghost of President Lincoln's son Willie, who had also been sighted by White House staff members in the Grant administration almost one hundred years earlier.

THE THING

In 1911, the spirit of an unidentified fifteen-year-old boy known as "the Thing" was said to have frightened the White

House staff. President William Howard Taft's aide told his sister that the White House was haunted. This ghost showed itself as a feeling of pressure on the shoulder, as if someone were standing right behind you.

When Taft heard whispers about the Thing he became furious. He ordered that anyone repeating the stories be fired!

Indeed, the house has had so many residents, it's not surprising that it could be haunted.

"George and I both pored over biographies and histories of the men and women who had inhabited these walls," Laura Bush wrote in her memoir. "Our bedside tables were crowded with books about their lives."

Many presidents and first ladies have felt frustrated in the White House, but many also never want to leave!

* * *

Epilogue

The Residence—1600 Pennsylvania Avenue—is more than a place: it is a symbol of American democracy.

It is a living museum, home to thousands of historical objects and pieces of artwork.

It is an evolving building, always changing to meet the needs of its current residents.

It is the president's home, the Residence of the leader of the free world. When one president moves out of the White House and another moves in, it represents more than a change of address. Moving day is part of the peaceful transfer of power that is a cornerstone of the democratic process.

It is a place where workers forge lifelong friendships.

It is a private home where a tradition of public service brings together a diverse group of professionals who are there for each other in good times and in bad, representing the best of our nation. The White House staff knows that they work for the office of the presidency rather than the individual holding the office.

Someone who exemplifies this tradition is James Jeffries, who is a witness to American history. He was either related to or knew most of the people who ran the Residence over the last fifty years. Nine members of his family worked at the White House, and he continued that tradition. He started working there on January 25, 1959, when he was just seventeen years old. He is one of a handful of people still alive who remembers what it was like to work as far back as the Eisenhower White House. His son is now a White House butler, and even though Jeffries himself is long past retirement age, he still works at "the house" part-time.

It is amazing that there are still Residence workers who actually hold dear firsthand personal memories of the Kennedys and Johnsons, the Nixons, Fords, Carters, and Reagans. Their recollections paint these famous figures in an intimate light. The Residence workers catch a glimpse of the humanity in the presidents and first ladies whose true personalities are rarely known beyond the walls of the White House. Just like anyone else, America's leaders have moments of indecision, exhaustion, frustration, and joy.

The Residence staff are bound together because they are, after all, the only people in the White House with no motivation other than to serve and comfort the first family. Without them, the White House would be uninhabitable. From preparing quiet meals for the first family to serving celebrities, members of Congress, and world leaders, they represent the best in American service, while practicing their own special brand of diplomacy. And their efforts are rewarded with the gratitude of the most powerful men and women on earth.

★ ★ ★

Acknowledgments

I want to thank the men and women who devote their lives to preserving the beauty and history of the White House. They are the heroes of this story and I am grateful that dozens of them took the time to talk to me about their incredible experiences.

★ ★ ★

White House Timeline

1790: Congress votes to build a house and office for the president.

1792: White House construction begins.

1800: John Adams and his wife, Abigail, become the first president and first lady to live in the White House.

1814: During the War of 1812, British troops burn the White House to the ground.

1817: James Monroe becomes the first president to move in after the fire.

1833: Running water is installed in the White House.

1871: The first state dinner is hosted by President Ulysses S. Grant.

1879: A telephone is installed in the White House.

1890–1965: Jim Crow Laws, which affected where African Americans could live and work, were in place.

1891: Electricity is installed in the White House.

1902: President Theodore Roosevelt hires famed New York architects McKim, Mead & White to renovate the White House, moving his office from the second floor of the Residence into the West Wing.

1909: President William Taft expands the West Wing and adds the Oval Office.

1920: The Nineteenth Amendment passes, giving women the right to vote.

1927: A third floor is added to the White House.

1934: The East Wing is built, including offices, a bomb shelter, and a movie theater.

1952: President Harry Truman completely guts the White House and renovates, adding the Truman Balcony overlooking the South Lawn. He and his family live temporarily at Blair House, across Pennsylvania Avenue from the White House, during construction.

1954–1968: The civil rights movement

1961: The Kennedy family move into the White House, including John F. Kennedy Jr., who is just two months old, and Caroline, who is three.

1963: President John F. Kennedy is shot by Lee Harvey Oswald during a trip to Dallas, Texas, making him the fourth president assassinated in office.

1974: President Richard Nixon resigns because of his involvement in Watergate. He is the first, and only, president to ever resign.

1992: The White House is wired for the internet.

2001: On September 11, the terrorist group al-Qaeda attacks the United States. Two airplanes crash into the twin towers in New York City, a plane crashes into the Pentagon in Washington, D.C., and United Airlines Flight 93 crashes in a field near Shanksville, Pennsylvania. It is thought to have been headed to the White House or the Capitol.

2008: Barack Obama becomes the first African American elected president of the United States. He and his wife, Michelle, and their two daughters, Sasha and Malia, are the first African American family to make the White House their home.

2016: Donald Trump is elected the forty-fifth president of the United States. Trump's wife, Melania, who was born in Slovenia, becomes the first first lady born outside the U.S. since Louisa Adams, who was born in London in 1775. The Trumps' son, Barron, is the first boy to live in the White House since newborn John F. Kennedy Jr. moved into the executive mansion with his family in 1961.

2020: Joe Biden is elected the forty-sixth president of the United States. His wife, Dr. Jill Biden, becomes the first first lady to have a full-time job when she decides to continue her career as a college professor. Biden's vice president, Kamala Harris, becomes the first woman, the first black person, and the first person of South Asian descent to hold the office.

★ ★ ★

Questions to Get You Thinking

1. Do you think *Exploring the White House* does a good job of showing what it's like to work at the White House?
2. Which president and first lady had the best relationship with the Residence staff, and why?
3. What was the main message or theme of the book?
4. Was there a chapter or passage that especially helped you understand what it would be like to live in the White House?
5. Was there one butler, maid, chef, or florist whom you would like to meet?
6. Did this book make you want to live in the White House?
7. What did you learn from this book that you didn't know before?
8. Which is your favorite Secret Service code name? If you were president, what would you want your code name to be?
9. Which president and first lady had the best pet?
10. Do you think the Residence staff should stay on from one administration to the next, or do you think they should change with each new president?
11. If you were a member of the Residence staff, what job do you think you'd enjoy most?
12. If you could meet the child of any U.S. president, who would it be and why?

★ ★ ★

Presidents and First Ladies

George Washington & Martha Washington
1789 to 1797

John Adams & Abigail Adams
1797 to 1801

Thomas Jefferson & Martha Jefferson Randolph (his daughter)
1801 to 1809

James Madison & Dolley Madison
1809 to 1817

James Monroe & Elizabeth Monroe
1817 to 1825

John Quincy Adams & Louisa Adams
1825 to 1829

Andrew Jackson & Emily Donelson (his niece)
1829 to 1837

Martin Van Buren & Angelica Van Buren (his daughter-in-law)
1837 to 1841

William Henry Harrison & Anna Harrison
1841 to 1841

John Tyler & Letitia Tyler (his first wife); Priscilla Tyler (his
daughter-in-law); Letitia Tyler Semple (his daughter);
Julia Tyler (his second wife)
1841 to 1845

James K. Polk & Sarah Polk
1845 to 1849

Zachary Taylor & Margaret Taylor (his wife);
Mary Elizabeth Taylor Bliss (his daughter)
1849 to 1850

Millard Fillmore & Abigail Fillmore (his wife);
Mary Abigail Fillmore (his daughter)
1850 to 1853

Franklin Pierce & Jane Pierce
1853 to 1857

James Buchanan & Harriet Lane (his niece)
1857 to 1861

Abraham Lincoln & Mary Todd Lincoln
1861 to 1865

Andrew Johnson & Eliza Johnson (his wife);
Martha Johnson Patterson (his daughter)
1865 to 1869

Ulysses S. Grant & Julia Grant
1869 to 1877

Rutherford B. Hayes & Lucy Hayes
1877 to 1881

James A. Garfield & Lucretia Garfield
1881 to 1881

Chester A. Arthur & Mary McElroy (his sister)
1881 to 1885

Grover Cleveland & Rose Cleveland (his sister);
Frances Cleveland (his wife)
1885 to 1889

Benjamin Harrison & Caroline Harrison (his wife);
Mary Harrison McKee (his daughter)
1889 to 1893

Grover Cleveland & Frances Cleveland
1893 to 1897

William McKinley & Ida McKinley
1897 to 1901

Theodore Roosevelt & Edith Roosevelt
1901 to 1909

William Howard Taft & Helen Taft
1909 to 1913

Woodrow Wilson & Ellen Wilson (his wife);
Margaret Wilson (his daughter); Edith Wilson (his second wife)
1913 to 1921

Warren G. Harding & Florence Harding
1921 to 1923

Calvin Coolidge & Grace Coolidge
1923 to 1929

Herbert Hoover & Lou Hoover
1929 to 1933

Franklin D. Roosevelt & Eleanor Roosevelt
1933 to 1945

Harry S. Truman & Bess Truman
1945 to 1953

Dwight D. Eisenhower & Mamie Eisenhower
1953 to 1961

John F. Kennedy & Jacqueline Kennedy
1961 to 1963

Lyndon B. Johnson & Claudia Alta "Lady Bird" Johnson
1963 to 1969

Richard M. Nixon & Thelma Catherine "Pat" Nixon
1969 to 1974

Gerald R. Ford & Elizabeth Anne "Betty" Ford
1974 to 1977

Jimmy Carter & Rosalynn Carter
1977 to 1981

Ronald Reagan & Nancy Reagan
1981 to 1989

George H. W. Bush & Barbara Bush
1989 to 1993

Bill Clinton & Hillary Clinton
1993 to 2001

George W. Bush & Laura Bush
2001 to 2009

Barack Obama & Michelle Obama
2009 to 2017

Donald J. Trump & Melania Trump
2017 to 2021

Joseph R. Biden Jr. & Dr. Jill Biden
2021 to present

Selected Bibliography

Anthony, Carl Sferrazza. *America's First Families: An Inside View of 200 Years of Private Life in the White House.* New York: Touchstone, 2000.

Baldrige, Letitia. *A Lady, First: My Life in the Kennedy White House and the American Embassies of Paris and Rome.* New York: Viking Penguin, 2001.

Brower, Kate Andersen. *The Residence: Inside the Private World of the White House.* New York: HarperCollins, 2015.

———. *First Women: The Grace and Power of America's Modern First Ladies.* New York: HarperCollins, 2016.

Bruce, Preston. *From the Door of the White House.* New York: Lothrop, Lee & Shepard Books, 1984.

Bryant, Traphes, with Frances Spatz Leighton. *Dog Days at the White House: The Outrageous Memoirs of the Presidential Kennel Keeper.* New York: Macmillan, 1975.

Bush, Barbara. *Barbara Bush: A Memoir.* New York: Scribner, 1994.

———. *Millie's Book: As Dictated to Barbara Bush.* New York: William Morrow, 1990.

Bush, George. *All the Best, George Bush: My Life in Letters and Other Writings.* New York: Scribner, 1999.

Bush, Laura. *Spoken from the Heart.* New York: Scribner, 2010.

Caro, Robert A. *The Passage of Power: The Years of Lyndon Johnson.* New York: Knopf, 2012.

Carpenter, Liz. *Ruffles and Flourishes: The Warm and Tender Story of a*

Simple Girl Who Found Adventure in the White House. Garden City, NY: Doubleday, 1970.

Carter, Jimmy. *Keeping Faith: Memoirs of a President.* Toronto; New York: Bantam Books, 1982.

Clinton, Bill. *My Life.* New York: Knopf, 2004.

Clinton, Catherine. *Mrs. Lincoln: A Life.* New York: Harper Perennial, 2010.

Clinton, Hillary Rodham. *An Invitation to the White House: At Home with History.* New York: Simon & Schuster, 2000.

Eisenhower, Julie Nixon. *Pat Nixon: The Untold Story.* New York: Simon & Schuster, 2007.

Fields, Alonzo. *My 21 Years in the White House.* New York: Coward-McCann, 1961.

Ford, Betty, with Chris Chase. *The Times of My Life.* New York: Harper & Row, 1978.

Ford, Gerald R. *A Time to Heal: The Autobiography of Gerald R. Ford.* New York: Harper & Row, 1979.

Gibbs, Nancy, and Michael Duffy. *The Presidents Club: Inside the World's Most Exclusive Fraternity.* New York: Simon & Schuster, 2012.

Johnson, Lady Bird. *A White House Diary.* New York: Holt, Rinehart and Winston, 1970.

Kantor, Jodi. *The Obamas.* New York: Little, Brown, 2012.

Klara, Robert. *The Hidden White House: Harry Truman and the Reconstruction of America's Most Famous Residence.* New York: Thomas Dunne Books, 2013.

Mesnier, Roland, with Christian Malard. *All the President's Pastries: Twenty-Five Years in the White House.* Paris: Flammarion, SA, 2006.

Obama, Barack. *The Audacity of Hope: Thoughts on Reclaiming the*

American Dream. New York: Crown, 2006.

Obama, Michelle. *Becoming.* New York: Crown, 2018.

Parks, Lillian Rogers, with Frances Spatz Leighton. *My Thirty Years Backstairs at the White House.* New York: Fleet, 1961.

Schifando, Peter, and J. Jonathan Joseph. *Entertaining at the White House with Nancy Reagan.* New York: William Morrow, 2007.

Seale, William. *The President's House: A History.* Vols I and II. Washington, D.C.: White House Historical Association with the Cooperation of the National Geographic Society, 1986.

———. "Secret Spaces at the White House?" *White House History* 29 (Summer 2011).

Slevin, Peter. *Michelle Obama: A Life.* New York: Vintage, 2016.

Smith, Sally Bedell. *Grace and Power: The Private World of the Kennedy White House.* New York: Random House, 2004.

Wead, Doug. *All the Presidents' Children: Triumph and Tragedy in the Lives of America's First Families.* New York: Atria Books, 2003.

Weidenfeld, Sheila Rabb. *First Lady's Lady: With the Fords at the White House.* New York: Putnam, 1979.

West, J. B., with Mary Lynn Kotz. *Upstairs at the White House: My Life with the First Ladies.* New York: Coward, McCann & Geoghegan, 1973.

Whitcomb, John, and Claire Whitcomb. *Real Life at the White House: Two Hundred Years of Daily Life at America's Most Famous Residence.* New York: Routledge, 2000.

Woodward, Bob, and Carl Bernstein. *The Final Days.* New York: Simon & Schuster, 1976.

Recommended Reading

Angelo, Bonnie. *First Families: The Impact of the White House on Their Lives*. New York: Morrow, 2005.

Bausum, Ann. *Our Country's Presidents: A Complete Encyclopedia of the U.S. Presidency*. Washington, D.C.: National Geographic, 2017.

Brower, Kate Andersen. *First Women: The Grace and Power of America's Modern First Ladies*. New York: Harper, 2016.

Brower, Kate Andersen. *The Residence: Inside the Private World of The White House*. New York: Harper, 2015.

Bruce, Preston. *From the Door of the White House*. New York: Lothrop, Lee & Shepard Books, 1984.

Bush, Barbara. *Millie's Book: As Dictated to Barbara Bush*. New York: William Morrow, 1990.

Fields, Alonzo. *My 21 Years in the White House*. New York: Coward-Mc-Cann, 1961.

Flynn, Sarah Wassner. *1,000 Facts About the White House*. Washington, D.C.: National Geographic, 2017.

Grove, Noel, with William B. Bushong and Joel D. Treese. *Inside the White House: Stories from the World's Most Famous Residence*. Washington, D.C.: National Geographic, 2013.

Johnson, Lady Bird. *A White House Diary*. New York: Holt, Rinehart and Winston, 1970.

Kurtz, Howard M. *White House Pets*. Washington, D.C.: White House Historical Association, 2008.

Monkman, Betty C. *The Living White House*, 12th ed., Washington,

D.C.: White House Historical Association, 2007.

—————. *The White House: Its Historic Furnishings and First Families.* Washington, D.C.: White House Historical Association, 2000.

Pickens, Jennifer B. *Pets at the White House: 50 Years of Presidents and Their Pets.* Dallas, TX: Fife & Drum Press, 2012.

Rhatigan, Joe. *White House Kids: The Perks, Pleasures, Problems, and Pratfalls of the Presidents' Children.* Watertown, MA: Charlesbridge, 2012.

West, J. B., with Mary Lynn Kotz. *Upstairs at the White House: My Life with the First Ladies.* New York: Coward, McCann & Geoghegan, 1973.

★ ★ ★

Chapter Notes

INTRODUCTION

". . . a public fishbowl.": Marylou Tousignant, "A Boy Makes His Home at White House for First Time in a Half-Century," *Washington Post*, November 29, 2016.

1 1600 PENNSYLVANIA AVENUE: THE MOST FAMOUS HOUSE IN THE COUNTRY

". . . felt more certain that I was doing right, than I do in signing this paper.": Daniel J. Vermilya, "The Emancipation Proclamation," National Park Service, updated August 15, 2017, https://www.nps.gov /articles/the-emancipation-proclamation.htm.

"The White House is built on a human scale . . . looked small!": Author interview with Tricia Nixon Cox.

"It's the hardest room to clean . . . we just dreaded it.": Author interview with Betty Finney.

"We have not the least fence, yard, or other convenience . . . The principal stairs are not up, and will not be this winter.": Charles Hurd, "The White House; Presidential mansion, opening again to tourists, has been a housing problem for all its 146 years," *Life*, October 14, 1946.

"like a very, very fancy New York apartment . . . it's your home.": Author interview with Katie Johnson.

"When the room was to be cleaned . . . standing duty while the cleaner mopped the floor.": J. B. West with Mary Lynn Kotz, *Upstairs at the White House: My Life with the First Ladies* (New York: Coward, McCann & Geoghegan, 1973).

2 ON THE JOB: WORKING IN THE WHITE HOUSE

". . . the most powerful man in Washington, next to the president.":
West, *Upstairs at the White House*.

"The White House staff works together to keep . . . perfect as possible.": Author interview with Bob Scanlan.

"If a flower was down in an arrangement . . . on everybody.": Author interview with Bob Scanlan.

"It's almost like an addiction . . . It's not only about the place, it's about the people too.": Author interview with Bob Scanlan.

"When you become part of that house and you are a florist . . . It's not just the first family's, it's the public's too. We're doing flowers for the country.": Author interview with Bob Scanlan.

"What always struck me was the flowers . . . it's another thing to be sprucing things up in areas where people aren't even going to congregate.": Author interview with Reid Cherlin.

"The jobs in the White House are not advertised . . . recommended them for the job.": Author interview with Tony Savoy.

3 TRUE PROFESSIONALS: LOYALTY TO THE FIRST FAMILY

"What would you like to drink? . . . when sad things happened to either one of us, we were supportive.": Author interview with Barbara Bush.

"Your Majesty, would you care for a cocktail? . . . It blows your mind.": Author interview with Lynwood Westray.

"These are not political appointees . . . beautiful dinner.": Author interview with Laura Bush.

"We knew that any state dinner . . . own countries.": Author interview with Laura Bush.

"If you're having a little bit of a bad day . . . straight, and I could deal with the next day.": Author interview with Christine Limerick.

"I've gotten myself into something. Can you help me get out of it?":
West with Kotz, *Upstairs at the White House*.

"Bring drop cloths . . . Oh yes, and bring a stepladder.": West with
Kotz, *Upstairs at the White House*.

"This is where you would have spent the night if Jackie hadn't been
redecorating again.": West with Kotz, *Upstairs at the White House*.

"We always beat him, until the end. The last year we were there,
he and Marvin won the championship.": Author interview with Linsey
Little.

"By the time they got there . . . we just want to get back to our horseshoe tournament!'": Author interview with Worthington White.

"Okay, okay, okay . . .": Author interview with Worthington White.

"There is no way my wife is going to believe . . . Come with me."
Author interview with Frank Ruta.

"I would never ever *ever* say hello . . . it's rude not to say hello back.":
Author interview with Joel Jensen.

"You have a balance between serving the family and knowing when
you need to get out of their way . . . it was time to vacate the premises.":
Author interview with Christine Limerick.

"I'm just like a ghost . . . and you don't say nothing.": Author interview with Cletus Clark.

"It was rough . . . I can't stay here.": Author interview with James
Ramsey.

"Do you have a [criminal] record? . . . hire you with *any* kind of
record.": Author interview with James Ramsey.

"I passed the White House going to the Kennedy-Warren . . . would
be working in that place?'": Author interview with James Ramsey.

"He talked to me like I was his son.": Author interview with James
Ramsey.

"They are the greatest con artists in the world . . . feel they love them
best.": Author interview with Luci Baines Johnson.

"Jenna, Barbara—I loved them to death . . . I ain't that old, am I?'": Author interview with James Ramsey.

"He made them laugh . . . We thank God that James Ramsey was in our life.": Laura Bush speaking at James Ramsey's funeral.

"I didn't raise my daughter to be a toilet bowl cleaner . . . the toilet bowl cleaner for the White House. *How do you feel about that*?'": Author interview with Christine Limerick.

"I think she was worried I might become a spinster . . . the joke is that housekeepers come in trying to find a husband.": Author interview with Christine Limerick.

"We lost a friend, a very close friend.": Author interview with Nelson Pierce.

"To this day I can still feel the shock that ran through my whole body.": Preston Bruce, *From the Door of the White House* (New York: Lothrop, Lee & Shepard Books, 1984).

"'Bruce, you waited until we came.' . . . 'Yes.'": Bruce, *From the Door of the White House.*

"The president would have wanted you to have this.": Bruce, *From the Door of the White House.*

"Keep these gloves, and remember always that I wore them to my brother's funeral.": Bruce, *From the Door of the White House.*

". . . just broke apart.": Author interview with Bill Cliber.

"How can they say such awful things about my father?": Bruce. *From the Door of the White House.*

". . . positive spirit . . . true person.": Author interview with Tricia Nixon Cox.

"Mr. President, this is a time in my life that I wish had never happened . . .": Bruce, *From the Door of the White House.*

"I have in you a true friend.": Bruce. *From the Door of the White House.*

"Sometimes we would have a dinner . . . he would come in and he would say, 'Hey, fellas. You all did a good job tonight.'": Author interview with Herman Thompson.

"worked a two-day shift . . . Then his second day started.": Author interview with Lynda Bird Johnson Robb.

"It was three . . . we'd leave work.": Author interview Nelson Pierce.

"Who turned off the light? . . . I was finishing the frames for all those pictures you sent over.": Isaac Avery's oral history can be found at the John F. Kennedy Presidential Library and Museum at the University of Massachusetts Boston.

"He just went after him profusely.": Author interview with Bill Cliber.

"Well, you just do that. . . . on if you'd get here on time . . . Of course after that he didn't say any more to me.": Zephyr Wright's oral history can be found at the LBJ Presidential Library at the University of Texas at Austin.

"Mr. West, if you can't get that shower of mine fixed, I'm going to have to move back to the Elms.": West with Kotz. *Upstairs at the White House*.

"I guess you've been told about the shower . . . satisfied with what's left.": West with Kotz. *Upstairs at the White House*.

"Get rid of this stuff.": Frederick N. Rasmussen, "Howard B. 'Reds' Arrington," *Baltimore Sun*, March 27, 2007.

4 UNDERSTANDING THE PAST: RACE AND THE WHITE HOUSE

"In essence, the African American fingerprint has been on the White House since its inception.": Author interview with Lonnie Bunch.

"People are going to be careful about the way they treat you . . . You can see yourself sailing out of the gate if you're disrespectful.": Author interview with Charles Allen.

". . . was one place where you didn't have all that foolishness . . . people thought more of us because there we all were meeting kings and queens.": Author interview with Lynwood Westray.

"One day he caught a cab to go home and he told the guy . . .": Author interview with Lynwood Westray.

"That is the story of this country . . . black young women playing with their dogs on the White House lawn.": Michelle Obama speaking at the 2016 Democratic National Convention in Philadelphia, July 25, 2016.

". . . they look at Malia and Sasha and they say, 'Well, this looks like my grandbaby, or this looks like my daughter.'" Peter Slevin, *Michelle Obama: A Life* (New York: Vintage, 2016).

". . . came back into the [second floor] kitchen where we were, walked up beside me, tapped me on the shoulder and asked me . . . 'I ain't got to wait until tomorrow, I can do that right now. Congratulations!'": Author interview with James Jeffries.

"Oh, Bruce . . . I wish I were out there with them!": Bruce. *From the Door of the White House.*

"It was 'Mr. Allen' . . . She was not about to have them say 'Bruce' or 'Allen.'": Author interview with Jim Ketchum.

" . . . went by like a dream.": Bruce. *From the Door of the White House.*

5 SAFETY FIRST: SECRETS OF THE SECRET SERVICE

"secret people": Michelle Obama, *Becoming* (New York: Crown, 2018).

" . . . .stone-faced softies.": Obama, *Becoming.*

During a Republican primary debate in 2015, Donald Trump said that if he received Secret Service protection his code name would be "Humble." Instead, when he was actually given Secret Service protection and he was presented with a list of names beginning with the letter "M," Trump picked the name "Mogul." Jenna Johnson and Carol D. Leonnig, "Donald Trump's Secret Service Code Name Is Less Humble, More Mogul," *Washington Post*, November 10, 2015.

"The worst will be saying good-bye to the staff today, but if I lose it, too bad, they've been a part of our lives and they know we care . . . first walked in here.": George Bush, *All the Best, George Bush: My Life in Letters and Other Writings* (New York: Touchstone, 1999).

"We were too choked up with emotion to say what we felt . . . From then on it was all downhill. The hard part for me was over.": Barbara Bush, *A Memoir: Barbara Bush* (New York: Scribner, 1994).

"When the Clintons came down and Chelsea came with them . . . The whole room just broke up.": Author interview with Christine Limerick.

". . . moves 'em in and moves 'em out.": Author interview with Tony Savoy.

"This is the team I walked in the door with . . . they're the ones that make this place tick. We are on *their* ground now.": Author interview with Katie McCormick Lelyveld.

"At the time . . . *We* were the new kids.": Author interview with Katie McCormick Lelyveld.

"There are thousands of things like that running through your mind . . . to call up and say, 'I hate this'?": Author interview with Bob Scanlan.

"What's wrong with them?": Author interview with Bill Hamilton.

"I never made an angel food cake with strawberry in the hole! . . . forget about what they used to have!": Author interview with Roland Mesnier.

"If it was a call for the first lady, we'd put a little key . . . Chelsea would have three short rings.": Author interview with Skip Allen.

"The Residence staff knows when the comfortableness gets to the point where we can all collectively say, 'Ahhhhhh' . . . . we know we have proven that we can be trusted.": Author interview with Gary Walters.

"There are certain conveniences . . . someone who's in charge of figuring out your dinner plans.": Author interview with Katie McCormick
Lelyveld.

" . . . seemed to add up quickly, especially given the fancy-hotel quality of everything . . . would we realize that some of these items were
being flown in at great expense from overseas.": Obama, *Becoming*.

"We went to the grocery store every day.": Author interview with
Joel Jensen.

"If you didn't know who I was and I walked by you in the aisle, you
would have no idea what I'm picking up. Whatever you would buy at
home that you need, we pick up because they can't go out.": Author
interview with Joel Jensen.

"I loved Nancy Reagan. . . She knew what she wanted.": Author
interview with Joel Jensen.

". . . it was always delivered to me, it was never delivered to her. Then
I would take it into her room.": Author interview with Jane Erkenbeck.

". . . each and every . . .": Author interview with Gary Walters.

". . . run this place just like you'd run it for the *chintziest* [cheapest]
president who ever got elected! . . . as you read in the papers!": West with
Kotz. *Upstairs at the White House*.

"I saw the number and I was like . . . and say, 'You know what, this
seems about right.'": Author interview with Reggie Love.

"You need to be aware that when you have a bunch of friends over I
do see this.": Author interview with Susan Ford.

"It doesn't sound like very much, but that was enormous to me back
in '76!": Author interview with Rosalynn Carter.

"Chef, did you really need that many people to produce that event . . .
How do you think that discussion's going to go?": Author interview
with Walter Scheib.

"Our goal was to make sure that the first family was never embarrassed.": Author interview with Walter Scheib.

"If they were shocked, there's something wrong with them . . . I thought it was very cheap to live at the White House! I'd like to go back and live there and not have the responsibility.": Author interview with Barbara Bush.

"The president loved soup before he went to bed . . . had trouble with the can opener *again* last night.": Anne Lincoln's oral history is available at the John F. Kennedy Presidential Library and Museum.

"We had to go out and pick flowers to do dinners. We would go to the city parks to cut flowers.": Author interview with Ronn Payne.

"Police would actually stop us . . . of jail for picking daffodils on that big hillside in Rock Creek Park to do a dinner.": Author interview with Ronn Payne.

"We'd buy dried flowers from the market, or we'd have our garden-club ladies dry their own garden flowers, and that's what we had to use.": Author interview with Ronn Payne.

"It's the only time I ever had a job quit me . . . You had to relearn your job literally in an afternoon.": Author interview with Walter Scheib.

"There is no one more important . . . we were it.": Author interview with Roland Mesnier.

" . . . are so expensive they're like gold, like caviar.": Author interview with Roland Mesnier.

"I don't care what you do with yours . . . I'm willing to die for that!": Author interview with Roland Mesnier.

"I made many, many mocha cakes . . . . 'Roland, can I have a mocha cake tonight?'": Author interview with Roland Mesnier.

"'I think the roast beef should go here'—she'd point—'and I think it would look better if the peas were on this side.'": Author interview with Skip Allen.

" . . . watch out . . . If it was really bad, if she was expecting asparagus and got green beans, you had to have a good excuse.": Author interview with Skip Allen.

"Roland, I'm sorry but that's not going to do again . . . not your concern.": Author interview with Roland Mesnier.

"Mrs. Reagan, this is very nice and very beautiful . . .": Author interview with Roland Mesnier.

"Roland, you have two *days* and two *nights* before the dinner.": Author interview with Roland Mesnier.

"You say, 'Thank you, madam, for the wonderful idea.' You click your heels, turn around, and go to work.": Author interview with Roland Mesnier.

"I thought, *I can make it happen.* This is how you measure a person, when you're trapped like this: How is that person going to make it happen? You do whatever it takes.": Author interview with Roland Mesnier.

"Nancy Reagan and her social secretary came into . . . afternoon lunch, and for the state dinner. Every single flower, three times, every one.": Author interview with Ronn Payne.

8 A UNIQUE ROLE: AMERICA'S FIRST LADIES

"You are constitutionally required to be perfect.": A Texas woman's letter to First Lady Betty Ford, Cokie Roberts's oral history can be found at the Gerald R. Ford Presidential Foundation in Grand Rapids, Michigan.

". . . showman and a salesman, a clotheshorse and a publicity sounding board, with a good heart, and a real interest in the folks.": Lady Bird Johnson, *A White House Diary* (New York: Holt, Rinehart & Winston, 1970).

"If the first ladies were happy, I was happy.": Author interview with Christine Limerick.

"She'd be on the phone like a teenager. And when we saw that, we knew she was at peace, everything was good with her.": Author interview with Christine Limerick.

"That's when we knew they were as close to having a normal life as possible and that's what we tried to help them accomplish.": Author interview with Christine Limerick.

"I never, of course, liked the criticism . . . so why not do what you wanted to do.": Author interview with Rosalynn Carter.

"You wonder what must be going through their minds . . . I love the house when it's empty. It's my favorite time to walk around and listen to the ghosts.": Author interview with Christine Limerick.

"All these people come to see the White House and they see practically nothing that dates back before 1948 . . . and that has nothing to do with decoration. That is a question of scholarship.": Jacqueline Kennedy interview with Hugh Sidey, *Life*, September 1, 1961.

"most perfect house" in the country: Jacqueline Kennedy interview, *Life*.

"If there's anything I can't stand, it's Victorian mirrors—they're hideous. Off to the dungeons with them." West with Kotz, *Upstairs at the White House*.

"When you pick up the plate, you ask for the knife and the fork, and if it's not there, I say, 'Oh, maybe you dropped it.' We look around on the floor and they usually say, 'Well, here it is!'": Author interview with Skip Allen.

"People come here with the idea that this is their property, so they just help themselves.": Anne Lincoln's oral history is available at the John F. Kennedy Presidential Library and Museum.

"One night she saw one of the guests slip a vermeil knife into his pocket.": Anne Lincoln's oral history.

"When the final tally is taken, her contributions to our country will be bigger than mine.": James Cannon, *Gerald R. Ford: An Honorable Life* (Ann Arbor: University of Michigan Press, 2013).

"Watergate is the only crisis that ever got me down. It is just constant.": Julie Nixon Eisenhower. *Pat Nixon: The Untold Story*. New York:

Simon & Schuster, 2007.

"Pat Dear, this is not an engraved invitation . . . know please everything would be on the QT. Love, Mamie E": Private letters to Patricia Nixon can be found at the Richard Nixon Presidential Library and Museum in Yorba Linda, California.

"Chef, I have been eating all over the world, your food is the best.": Henry Haller interviewed for the Gerald R. Ford Oral History Project on March 31, 2010, by Richard Norton Smith.

"I was in the East Room painting the stage . . . I couldn't get out!": Author interview with Cletus Clark.

"This house has a great heart and that heart comes from those who serve. I was rather sorry they didn't come down . . . I might be a little down, but they always smiled.": President Richard Nixon's Final Remarks at the White House, August 9, 1974.

"The day President Nixon resigned, we went down to the White House, we met there for his resignation and Jerry Ford's swearing in hours later . . . waving good-bye while they changed the pictures.": Author interview with Barbara Bush.

"I knew there was wonderful furniture in the facility where the White House collection is stored and part of the fun . . . But you'll move out and some other family will move in.": Author interview with Laura Bush.

"the [Secret Service] agents ran in the building and told everyone to run from the White House . . . They just ran from the building, they didn't really know where to go.": Author interview with Laura Bush.

"We knew we were going to be there [in the White House] . . . .And they didn't, none of them did.": Author interview with Laura Bush.

"worldwide effort to focus . . . intimidate and control.": Presidential radio address, November 17, 2001.

". . . never forget the intense camaraderie and loyalty that the first ladies and members of the first ladies' staffs have for each other.": Author interview with Jackie Norris.

"What they wanted was to completely set aside . . . They were all in this unique position to understand just how hard her role would be.": Author interview with Jackie Norris.

"I'd never related to the story of John Quincy Adams . . . Eleanor Roosevelt or Mamie Eisenhower . . . I wanted to show up in the world in a way that honored who they were.": Obama, *Becoming*.

" . . . a different yardstick. . . . If there was a presumed grace assigned to my white predecessors, I knew it wasn't likely to be the same for me.": Obama, *Becoming*.

"Our culture has gotten too mean and too rough.": Sophie Tatum, "Melania Trump Thanks Chelsea Clinton for Defending Barron," CNN, August 23, 2017.

9 FIRST CHILDREN: GROWING UP IN THE WHITE HOUSE

" . . . a really nice prison.": Juliet Eilperin, "Michelle Obama Jokes: White House 'a Really Nice Prison,'" *Washington Post*, July 2, 2013.

"I don't think that any family has ever enjoyed the White House more than we have.": President Theodore Roosevelt in Marylou Tousignant, "A Boy Makes His Home at White House for First Time in a Half-Century," *Washington Post*, November 29, 2016.

"If you bungle raising your children, I don't think whatever else you do well matters very much.": Jacqueline Kennedy, www.jfklibrary.org /learn/about-jfk/life-of-jacqueline-b-kennedy

" . . . fluttering like little pink birds in their pink leotards, tulle tutus, and ballet slippers.": Letitia Baldrige, *A Lady, First: My Life in the Kennedy White House and the American Embassies of Paris and Rome* (New York: Viking Penguin, 2001).

"'She's grown so much, can you please take the blocks off?'. . . She was just so in love with those children. And she showed it.": Author interview with Larry Bush.

"Mr. Pierce, do somersaults with me!": Author interview with Nelson Pierce.

"My mother [Lady Bird Johnson] felt it was very appropriate that I help clean the smoke stains off the walls of my bedroom that first week.": Author interview with Luci Baines Johnson.

"The allegiance that the White House . . . makes you feel very proud to be an American.": Author interview with Luci Baines Johnson.

"All of a sudden we all got Secret Service agents . . . that's not really the group you're hoping to hang out with.": Author interview with Steve Ford.

"You gotta come over . . . You gotta see this place.": Author interview with Steve Ford.

"That was my first night in the White House . . . he never ratted me out to my parents. The staff knows everything you do.": Author interview with Steve Ford.

"The White House really belonged to the staff, because they were the ones who were there for four, five, six different administrations.": Author interview with Steve Ford.

"It was truly like living in a museum . . . 'Don't put your feet up there! That's Jefferson's table.'": Author interview with Steve Ford.

"Being a child growing up with adults, she learned to be just alone in her own little world no matter where she was.": Author interview with Rosalynn Carter.

"When I first got the call to go to the governor's mansion . . . From that day on, it was me and Amy.": Author interview with Mary Prince.

. . . Mary was "totally innocent" of the crime. "She had nothing to do with it.": Author interview with Rosalynn Carter.

"I was in the wrong place at the wrong time.": Author interview with Mary Prince.

"Hers was a story all too common . . . were imposed on our nation,": Jimmy Carter, *Keeping Faith: Memoirs of a President* (New York: Bantam Books, 1982).

"How would you like to work in this big old place?": Clare Crawford, "A Story of Love and Rehabilitation: The Ex-Con in the White House," *People*, March 14, 1977.

"Come on in! . . . just me and the first lady together out there swimming.": Author interview with Mary Prince.

"Teenagers, you're thinking rudeness. That was never, ever Chelsea . . . She wrote me a note thanking me for my services. That's just the way she was.": Author interview with Betty Finney.

"Mrs. Clinton had decided they wanted Chelsea to be a little bit more self-sufficient . . . So I got a call from Mrs. Clinton asking if I would teach Chelsea how to cook.": Author interview with Walter Scheib.

"She was an extremely quick study . . . She respected us tremendously in terms of us offering her our time.": Author interview with Walter Scheib.

"We know it wasn't always easy —the two of you and the two of us were teenagers trailed by men in backpacks—but they put their lives on hold for us.": Barbara Bush and Jenna Hager Bush, "The Bush Sisters Wrote the Obama Girls a Letter," *Time*, January 12, 2017.

"You have lived through the unbelievable pressure of the White House . . . who put you first and who not only showed you but gave you the world. As always, they will be rooting for you as you begin your next chapter. And so will we.": Bush and Bush, "The Bush Sisters."

"I love those girls . . . something and Chelsea would send a tweet out. That made a big, big difference.": Michelle Obama interview, *Good Morning America*, November 11, 2018.

" . . . wild little girls . . .": Author interview with Barbara Bush.

"We let them go in, even though the White House . . . little flower arrangements to bring up to us when we came in from the parade.": Author interview with Laura Bush.

"It's a miserable life for a teenager . . . you couldn't do anything without [the Secret Service] right on your tail.": Author interview with Nelson Pierce.

"You want your kids to grow up normal. You want them to be able to have wonderful experiences privately . . . they're not allowed to do that, it's unfair and you feel guilty about it. Because they didn't choose this life.": Michelle Obama interview, *Today*, November 14, 2018.

"I'm going home . . . still look good to me.": Author interview with Bob Scanlan.

"Daddy, there's no one on the road, I don't think anyone's coming to your celebration.": Michelle Obama, *Becoming*.

"Florist: I really like my tree. If it's not too much to ask could . . . Now you tell me, how could I *not* put lights on that tree?": Author interview with Bob Scanlan.

10 LIONS AND TIGERS AND BEARS, OH MY!: PETS IN THE WHITE HOUSE

"If you want a friend in Washington, get a dog.": "White House Pets: A President's Best Friend," White House Historical Association.

"Charlie, go get you a duck! . . . the president was laughing the whole time!": Author interview with Milton Frame.

"What does Clipper eat?": Carl Sferrazza Anthony, *America's First Families* (New York: Touchstone, 2000).

" . . . as if they were his distinguished hosts.": Traphes Bryant with Frances Spatz Leighton, *Dog Days at the White House* (New York: Macmillan, 1975).

"Oh, gosh," Bush told the president, "Millie kills squirrels!": Barbara Bush, *Millie's Book: As Dictated to Barbara Bush*. (New York: William Morrow, 1990).

"You are so nice, they are very dirty dogs.": Author interview with Barbara Bush.

"One of the ways I really relaxed when I was president was walking . . . It didn't matter rain or shine, he was at my side or sleeping on our bed . . . He was my friend and companion.": Anthony, *America's First Families*.

"Harold Hancock was one of the doorman . . . They acted like they were really wild about all the animals, whether they were or not.": Author interview with Laura Bush.

"He was Barney and Miss Beazley's best friend," she said. "They were in the White House garden with Dale every day.": Author interview with Laura Bush.

11 THINGS THAT GO BUMP IN THE NIGHT: WHITE HOUSE GHOSTS

"Nancy Reagan's dog Rex would bark outside the Lincoln Bedroom like there was a ghost in there. They'd shut the door and he'd still bark outside.": Author interview with Wendy Elsasser.

"He was sitting there with his legs crossed, he had a charcoal-gray pinstripe suit on . . . No expression at all.": Author interview with Betty Finney.

"I sit here in this old house and work on foreign affairs, read reports, and work on speeches—all the while listening to the ghosts walk up and down the hallway and even right here in the study. The floors pop and the drapes move back and forth.": Robert Klara, *The Hidden White House: Harry Truman and the Reconstruction of America's Most Famous Residence* (New York: Thomas Dunne Books, 2013).

"George and I both pored over . . . Our bedside tables were crowded with books about their lives.": Laura Bush, *Spoken from the Heart* (New York: Scribner, 2010).

EPILOGUE

works at "the house" part-time: Author interview with James Jeffries.

GRATEFUL ACKNOWLEDGMENT IS GIVEN TO THE FOLLOWING SOURCES FOR THE IMAGES IN THIS BOOK:

p. 16: Credit: White House Historical Association; p. 21: National Park Service; p. 25: Library of Congress, photographer: Harris & Ewing; p. 27: Library of Congress, photographer: Carol M. Highsmith; p. 28: Official White House photograph by D. Myles Cullen; p. 36: Official White House photograph by Shealah Craighead, courtesy of Bob Scanlan; p. 46: Tina Hager/White House, courtesy George W. Bush Presidential Library & Museum; p. 51: Official White House photograph, courtesy of Linsey Little; p. 53: Richard Nixon Presidential Library and Museum, photographer: Jack Kightlinger; p. 56: Tina Hager/White House, courtesy George W. Bush Presidential Library & Museum; p. 59: Official White House photograph, courtesy of Linsey Little; p. 60: Official White House photograph, courtesy of Christine Limerick; p. 67: Official White House photograph by Yoichi Okamoto, W98-30, LBJ Library; p. 70: Tina Hager/White House, courtesy George W. Bush Presidential Library & Museum; p. 71: Abbie Rowe/National Park Service, courtesy Margaret Arrington; p. 77: Library of Congress; p. 79: Ankers Capitol Photographers, courtesy of Lynwood Westray; p. 83: Robert Knudsen/White House, December 6, 1963, courtesy John F. Kennedy Presidential Library and Museum, Boston; p. 101: Official White House photograph, courtesy of Roland Mesnier; p. 102, Official White House photograph, courtesy of Skip Allen; p. 119: Pete Souza/White House, courtesy Ronn Payne; p. 134: Abbie Rowe. White House Photographs. John F. Kennedy Presidential Library and Museum, Boston; p. 137: Oliver Atkins/White House, courtesy Richard Nixon Presidential Library; p. 143: Barack Obama Presidential Library; p. 149: Cecil Stoughton/White House, John F. Kennedy Presidential Library and Museum, Boston; p. 150: Robert Knudsen/White House, December 19, 1963. John F. Kennedy Presidential Library and Museum, Boston; p. 156: National Archives, Gerald R. Ford Presidential Library and Museum; p. 158: Courtesy: Jimmy Carter Presidential Library; p. 160: Bill Fitz-Patrick/White House, courtesy Jimmy Carter Presidential Library and Museum; p. 169: White House Photo Office, photographer: Joyce N. Boghosian; p. 182: White House Photo Office, photographer: Joyce N. Boghosian; p. 190: Tina Hager/White House, courtesy George W. Bush Presidential Library & Museum